DISCLAIMER

No part of this Book may be reproduced or transmitted in any form or by any means, electronic or mechanical, including photocopying, recording or by any information storage and retrieval system, without written permission from the author.

While we try to keep the information up-to-date and correct, there are no representations or warranties, express or implied, of any kind and assume no labilities of any kind with respect to the completeness or accuracy, of the content. We explicitly disclaim any implied warranties of merchantability or fitness for a specific purpose. Any use of the methods describe within this Book are the author's personal thoughts. It is possible that you may find alternative techniques and resources to achieve the desired outcome. If the expertise of a professional is needed, it is advisable to seek the services of a qualified individual.

Names and persons in this book are entirely fictional. They bear no resemblance to anyone living or dead.

STOP
STRUGGLING FOR MONEY,
START
MAKING IT

Roadmap to Earn Money and More Money

SUKHVINDER SINGH

notionpress.com

INDIA • SINGAPORE • MALAYSIA

ISBN 979-8-89363-401-3

CONTENTS

INTRODUCTION

In life, there are only two options: either earn money for your needs and survival or become a monk. I don't think enough people have the option of becoming a monk. Hence, the only option left is to earn money. As far as earning money is concerned, either you earn it in the right way and become financially free, or you keep struggling throughout your life. For some, money can bring security and freedom; for others, it can be a source of endless stress and struggle.

Allow me to impart a brief financial maxim. Regardless of our career path—whether it is self-employment, business, or employment—if we do not achieve financial independence by the time we are 50, we are all basically labourers. Hence, it is important to emerge from this toil and ceaseless endeavour and learn those important aspects of finance that can make us financially free in our lives.

Being financially free does not imply that you stop earning money; rather, it implies that you stop struggling for money, stop taking stress for money, avoid doing things you dislike doing for money, and finally work on your own terms and conditions. Financial freedom means now money starts working for you and you just live your life the way you want. Financial independence refers to the state when one's wealth generates income, allowing individuals to live according to their desires without being constrained by financial obligations.

In addition to security, financial independence gives you the strength and flexibility to prioritize the things in life that matter most, such as your family, your passion, your health, your dreams, and your freedom. Instead of constantly worrying about the balance sheet of the firm, you strive for balance in your own life, spend quality time with your family, socialize in a healthy way, enjoy life rightfully, and live life which is a one-time opportunity, as you rightfully deserve.

However, the first step towards your financial freedom is mindset. Money will never come to your bank account; till the time your mindset makes it happen. Our minds are extremely complex. It's not just intricate, but if approached incorrectly, it may also become extremely rigid. Our minds are harder to shape than steel. That's why the first few chapters of this book deal with mindset.

This book will shatter your mental barriers, such as: I can't become wealthy because I'm poor; I can't become wealthy because I'm uneducated; I can't make money because the market isn't favourable; I can't succeed financially because I have debts; there is no hope in my life for financial success; since I am now retired. This book will obliterate all such mental barriers.

We also need to understand how to properly set our financial objectives. I have attempted to make everything plain and straightforward, using numerical data and illustrative examples.

Further how to find our motivation factor that drives us fervently towards financial freedom. What are the factors that motivate us. This book is not just about equations and concepts; but it will also motivate you and assist you in reaching your financial goals. This book contains real-life stories of rags to riches that you can relate to in your own life.

Finally, we need to learn how to make money. Not just money but more money, which means millions and billions.

The first step is to earn money, second to earn more money, Subsequently, one should engage in astute investing strategies, and finally, establish mechanisms for generating passive income.

    1. First Step   :   Earn Money.

    2. Second Step   :   Earn More Money

3. Third Step   :   Invest Money.

4. Fourth Step   :   Create means of Passive money.

The above four steps will not only make you wealthy but also help you to stay wealthy.

We are going to explore various equations and strategies that shall help all the individuals irrespective of any stream or status, to improve their financial status and finally become financially free in their life.

In this book, I have started with the basics. What exactly does it take to earn money?

With over a quarter-century of professional experience and three books to my name, I've dissected the anatomy of wealth to bring you the essence of financial growth. How does one earn money—and then more money? This question, simple yet profound, is the heart of our journey together. Through these pages, we will navigate the labyrinth of earning and the strategies that separate the affluent from the struggling masses. And perhaps you too will hear the subtle notes of prosperity.

With the knowledge of this book and the insights, it will help you to augment your personal wealth and achieve all that seemed to be impossible, financially.

As you traverse the chapters of this tome, you will be introduced to strategies both innovative and time-tested, designed to elevate you from the mire of financial uncertainty to the firm ground of monetary growth. The solutions and insights within these pages are distilled from years of observation, study, and personal triumphs. They are your compass and map as you navigate the complex terrain of economic gain.

As we embark on this journey together, prepare to be challenged, to have your preconceptions overturned, and your potential unleashed. It is time to step into the arena where money is not just earned but multiplied.

In the coming chapters, you will not find empty promises or vapid platitudes. Instead, you will discover practical advices, shared experiences, and actionable strategies. We will discuss the psychology of wealth, the mechanics of money-making, and the discipline of asset accumulation.

This book is not merely collections of pages but vaults of potential energy, waiting to be transformed into action and change lives of people who have will and determination to act.

So, dear reader, let us commence this expedition with resolve and anticipation. The secrets of earning money—and then more money—await your keen eyes and willing mind. Let the journey begin.

Life will be easy,

Once you are at ease with your own self,

provided

your stomach and wallet both are full.

BASICS

The nature of Life is like a slope of a hill. Either we move ahead towards success or life will make us fall automatically. Life does not hold us at any particular point forever. Similarly, the world is not waiting; it is hurtling forward, and to stand still is to fall behind.

Hence it is imperative that we learn the facts to grow & succeed so that we are not thrown back despite of our potential abilities.

We all have intrinsic abilities, skills, potential. However, we need the right direction and, a driving force to achieve the seemingly impossible task.

God has made everybody different, or, I would say, unique. It is not that somebody has more as compared to us, but we all have different features of potential. The fact is that some people have taken their ability to an unprecedented level, whereas some are yet to know it. We have to explore our unbeatable unique potential and accumulate all our energy to achieve our desired goals.

Very unfortunate are those who cannot see their hidden potential. More unfortunate people are those who know their potential but do not excel them. Successful people explore their own potential, derive them energetically and exert consistently, till they reach their destiny. They don't go and ask people to read their fate lines. They make their own destiny.

We are not meant to live at the mercy of our destiny, rather we should be determined to make our own destiny.

LIFE is a like a ground. It depends on how we use this valuable resource. I am citing one example to have a better understanding of my point of view.

A village had a considerable expanse of land. Due to the ample space available, all individuals were permitted to participate in their preferred activities. Mainly, there were four activities that were carried out:

First Activity: Few kids from the hamlet would come and play in that area. They used to spend much of their time playing, relaxing when they were exhausted, and then just hanging around, gossiping, and killing their time. Since they were children, this was their main activity.

Second Activity: There was a farmer who cultivated various crops on that land. The land was quite fertile, and the farmer was quite experienced too. He used to work hard to ensure a successful harvest. Finally, whatever he earned he just managed to make both ends meet.

Third Activity: There was another individual who was quite educated and had extensive experience working in the gold mines. When he saw this land, he discovered that it was not only good for farming but also had an abundant reserve of gold. With the right technique, he could extract gold from that land instead of farming. With all his experience and skills, he started the process of extracting gold. The land proved to be a lucrative resource, leading to substantial financial gains for him. He became a rich man.

Fourth Activity: Similar to the individuals mentioned above, there was one more person who realized that the land not only had gold but a lot of diamonds too if dug more deeply and precisely on certain spots. Having the skills to locate those spots, dig with precision, and with his ability to identify the diamonds, the man extracted a lot of diamonds. The land turned out to have a vast deposit of diamonds, and he became extremely wealthy.

Referring to the above, our lives are just like that land, which provides you with all the resources. However, the most important aspect is our attitude towards life. Some people play like the kids in the first activity because they believe that life should be enjoyed. They play, gossip, and spend time on social media, with their primary objective being to just derive pleasure from life. At the end, they achieve nothing except getting tired and returning home without any accomplishments. Ultimately, their lives become devoid of meaning.

Second is a farmer who is like a middle-class person, willing to work hard but does not have any special skills. Consequently, he leads a conventional life with constant hardships.

Third are the people with special skills. Owing to their exceptional abilities, they surpass the common man and amass wealth.

The extraordinary individuals with specialized skills make up the fourth category. They extract diamonds and enjoy all the splendour and luxuries of this world. They have acquired valuable skills and have the ability to identify the right opportunities. With a combination of their expertise and opportunities, they become the exceptional class of this world and rise to the top of the global hierarchy.

Well, it is for us to decide what activity we shall carry out in our lives. Shall we take our lives for enjoyment, or shall we become average men and toil throughout our lives? Shall we opt to cultivate some special skills or have exceptional expertise and become an extraordinary person? The most important thing here is our choice of goals and our attitude towards them. Our choice of goals will determine the quality of our lives, and our attitude will determine whether we will be able to achieve them or not.

"Your goals decide your destiny. Your attitude decides whether the goals are achievable or not."

Hence, choose your goals wisely and pursue them enthusiastically. In subsequent chapters, I have given detailed information on goal settings, which will help you to analyse your goals, assess their magnitude, and take key factors into consideration while you finally determine their significance. First and foremost, base your goals on values and synchronize them with your aptitude and financial priorities. The trajectory of your life will be determined by the objectives you set, ultimately shaping your life and identity in the long run.

OVERCOMING MENTAL BARRIERS TO BECOME A MILLIONAIRE

৵৽

To become a millionaire is a fervent wish of everyone. When I was young, this seemed like an impossible dream that could hardly be accomplished. Despite having a Bachelor's degree in Engineering and a Master's degree in Business Administration, I was unable to achieve financial success, and as time went on, I lost all hope that I would ever be wealthy. Sometimes education narrows our perspective in life, and our belief system makes it more rigid and unyielding.

Further, I had seen a lot of educated and intelligent people working hard and sincerely, but eventually all of them were leading mediocre lives. Despite having big dreams, their narrow beliefs about money took deep roots within their sub-conscious mind and limited their financial destinies. These beliefs, often inherited and unexamined, constrained their financial perspective, eventually acting as invisible barriers to financial prosperity.

But what if we could break free from these constraints? What if can dismantle these limiting beliefs and replacing them with empowering convictions? Will it open the doors to a world of financial empowerment and possibility?

Let us pause for a moment to reflect upon the gravity of our discussion.

Once, I happened to meet one of my friends named Rahul, while I was parking my car in the basement of a shopping mall. I knew him since childhood; basically, he belonged to a very poor family. It was unexpected to see him park his BMW. I was addled, and I wondered what happened—did he win some lottery?

As we were shaking hands and greeting each other, I asked him bluntly, "Rahul, is this your BMW?"

He said smilingly, "Yes of course it is mine, Sukhvinder."

I was again amazed and I asked him, "What are you doing?"

He said, "I am in a hurry right now. Shall we discuss this later."

I said, "Fine, whenever you feel free."

Suddenly he said, "Let's meet somewhere."

I was indeed curious to know about him, and I replied, "Ofcourse, it would be a pleasure seeing you again."

"Okay, then let's meet this Saturday at my house," he said right away. "We shall have dinner together. I'll send my address to you."

I agreed. We shared our mobile numbers and I was eager to see him again.

Finally, I was there at his house on Saturday. As imagined, it was a luxurious bungalow with upscale amenities, lavish décor, exotic interiors, and a perfectly sculpted garden with beautiful flowers. We were sitting in the garden, the cool breeze drifting through the plants and wafting the sweet smell of the flowers. It was like a paradise. Rahul was a teetotaller, and so was I. However, I was enjoying the soft drinks and the barbeques. Rahul was profuse in his hospitality.

We talked a lot about success. However, I was desperate to know about him and how he managed to become exceptionally rich despite belonging to a very poor family. So, I requested that he share his entire journey.

I am going to narrate the story in his own words.

He said, "Sukhvinder, you are already aware; we were very poor. I was brought up in an impoverished family, and right from the beginning, I had a goal to earn money. My father was a worker toiling in a small factory, and my mother was a housewife. I had two brothers and one sister, and we were living in a one-room house. So, earning money was utterly important in my life.

However, like a common man, I also thought that earning money was the most difficult task in this world. As far as my mindset was concerned, it was impoverished too, just like my circumstances. Hence, becoming a multi-millionaire was an impossible task in my life.

I definitely had the desire to become rich, but within the core of my mind were several barriers. Barriers that restricted my ability to grow. Like a common man, I also thought that it was not easy to earn money. Since I came from a poor background, it was almost impossible for me to become rich. I had practically nothing that could make me eligible to become rich. Since I had no special education and no experience, there was no hope of financial prosperity in my life. I always believed that there are millions of people much smarter than me; if they cannot become rich, how can I? My subconscious mind always used to whisper that it was impossible for a person like me to become rich. Hence, these barriers resided 24 hours, 365 days, within the core of my mind. I could never figure out how to break these barriers. Hence, despite having big dreams, I had a very negative mindset and a very low self-esteem. I would say there was absolutely no hope in my life.

Sukhvinder it was not that I was financially poor; the fact was that I was mentally even more poorer. Whenever I talked to my parents about becoming rich, they discouraged me by saying that these are fantasies like what we see in the movies, and they prodded me to leave all my dreams aside, which according to them were utterly meaningless. My parents strongly advised me to find a job, like my younger brother, who had already started working as an assistant in a shop.

Hence, my family support was totally disheartening. Considering my circumstances, my family background, my skills, my abilities, and finally my mindset, I was in a totally hopeless situation. There was absolutely no hope in my life and no means to achieve my dreams. We were indeed poor and just poor, by all means."

I asked him very curiously, "Rahul, how did things change then?"

He replied, "One day, I was going to my village, which is a one-hour journey by bus. I was waiting for the bus. The bus was late for 20 to 30 minutes. Coincidentally, there was an ascetic standing there, looking very charming and happy. He was going to some other village. It was a different route. He asked me which bus would take him there. I looked at the chart and gave him the bus number, which was scheduled to arrive within 15 minutes.

Since I was alone and getting bored, I started some conversation with him, asking where he lived.

"I am an ascetic; I don't belong to any specific place, family, caste, or country," he replied with a smirk. "I belong to the whole world."

He then became pensive for a while, and suddenly asked, what was I doing?

"I am doing nothing in my life," I retorted.

I also added, "I am a burden to my family and to my own life," in a very negative way.

He smiled and asked, "What makes you feel like that?"

Basically, I was so frustrated in my life that I wanted someone with whom I could share my feelings. Hence, I started blurting out all my frustrations.

I told him all that was going on within me—about my big dreams, about my circumstances, the discouragement from my family, and also about my mindset, which was in total despondency and despair. There was nothing in my life that encouraged me to move ahead. I shared with him all the disturbance and mess within me. For me, he was the right person, and it was the perfect opportunity to reveal all my vexations. Hence, I vomited all my disappointments, not for a solution but to relive myself."

In sheer audacity I also said, "Meeting God and earning money, are two impossible tasks in this world."

He once again smiled and said, "Well, as far as meeting God is concerned, believe me, it is the easiest task in this world, and so is earning money."

The moment he said that, I was amazed, as for the first time, I met a person who claims that meeting God is the easiest thing in this world.

So, I asked him impatiently, "You mean to say it is easy to meet God? I don't believe you."

He replied, "It doesn't matter what you believe and what you don't. It does not change the truth."

"Okay, tell me then how to meet God; tell me the way," I asked.

He replied, "No, first, you tell me what you want in your life. Do you want to become rich, or do you want to see God? What is it that you fervently desire?"

I immediately said, "I want to become rich."

He said, "No tell me specifically, how much money you intend to earn? Be specific."

I immediately replied, "I want to earn Rs. 15 crores (US $ 2 millions)."

He said, "Fine, then let's talk about money."

I again replied, "I am sorry, you are an ascetic. You don't know anything about finance. It is not your subject. I don't think you can help me in this matter."

He once again smiled and said, "I may not be a man of finance but I am a Yogi, which means I am a man of abundance. Whatever I desire flows into my life in abundance. Wealth is merely a small manifestation of abundance, just one expression of abundance. However, the source of this manifestation is not only within me but within all of us. An enlightened person realizes this truth, but the ignorant remains deprived. Hence, he remains poor and impoverished. Realize this truth, my boy, as this source of abundance, a wellspring of infinite potential, also lies within you. Embrace this potential, and you will get far more than you could have ever imagined."

The way he spoke I was stunned. There was poise and depth in his voice.

He continued, "My boy, earning money is a damn easy thing. It is your ignorance that is making it difficult for you. Just like a person sitting in the dark who cannot see anything around him, so is your situation. Due to your ignorance, you cannot see the wealth, the means, and the resources available in abundance around you."

I was really moved to what he said and I asked him, "Ok tell me, how earning money is easier in this world?"

He replied, "To become a millionaire is an easy task. If you don't believe me, then answer my question."

"What question?" startlingly I asked.

He replied, "How difficult do you think it is to fetch a drop of water from the ocean? Just a small drop of water from the ocean! Imagine standing at the edge of a vast ocean, the horizon stretching beyond the limits of sight. Now just to fetch a small drop of water from the ocean. How difficult do you think it is? Answer me, boy."

I replied, "Very Easy."

He said, "In comparison to the total wealth in this world, what is Rs. 15 crores? It is just nothing in contrast to the entire wealth of this globe. These Rs. 15 crores are but a tiny drop in comparison to the vast ocean of water. Still, you think it is difficult. Are you insane? It is only due to your ignorance; it seems difficult to you. My child, come out of this darkness."

What he said was right. He made a valid point. To earn this one drop of wealth, why did I consider it impossible? Even in more difficult situations, people just like me have succeeded; why can't I? People who were uneducated, impoverished, or even disabled have earned millions; why can't I? My desire for money is nothing more than a drop of water from the ocean.

I looked at him, he was smiling and lastly, he said, "Be positive in life, every human being has the potential to achieve whatever his mind determines. Nature has given infinite potential to human beings, beyond one's imagination, to achieve whatever he wants. It is only because of our ignorance that we cannot see the power that lies in abundance within us. Your mindset is the landscape where resources are infinite and possibilities are endless.

Your thought process, your assumptions, your beliefs, and your attitude have confined you and made you internally poor. They are restricting your ability to evolve and grow and are holding you back from achieving what you truly deserve.

I am sorry to say that you have become a self-discouraging person, like a common man and all these beliefs are self-imposed. Come out of this poverty. Your mind is not burdened because of your circumstances, but it is handcuffed because of your negative thinking.

Poor people are not the victims of their circumstances; they are victims of their poor mindset, which they dwell on throughout their lives and remain poor.

My son, believe in yourself; you have the potential to do miracles in your life. Once you accept this fact, it will open the door to a world of financial empowerment and infinite possibilities. You are a human being, not an ordinary being; you are the best creation of God. Don't evaluate yourself with your limited mindset or belief system. You have the potential to turn the impossible into the possible. It is only human beings who have the privilege to have dreams in their lives, and with this privilege, God has also given them immense potential to convert their dreams into reality. Don't undermine your powers; don't confine or limit yourself; wake up and realize your inner strength. Believe in your powers, which lie in abundance within you; make use of them, and you will realize you are a supernatural human being. The potential that nature has given you is much more than the strength of the mountains, the current of the oceans, and the power of storms.

Stay positive and stay determined; work hard; and whatever challenges may befall you, don't quit; don't even think to give up. Be persistent and consistent, and stay committed to your goals.

Realize your potential, unleash your powers, and believe in yourself, and you will become limitless. Then this Rs. 15 crore will be just like fetching a drop of water from the oceans. If you believe me, wealth will flow in abundance into your life. Mark my words, and you will see things happening, like a miracle in your life."

As he said this, his bus came. He moved on smilingly, but his body and soul were radiating all the truth with the speed of light, penetrating my mind and breaking all those barriers.

I was looking at him. His words sparked flames in my hopeless heart. His words were resonating within me. His words unlocked the doors to a new way of being.

As he said, "Believe in yourself, you have immense power within you, the potential which nature has given you is much more than the strength of the mountains, the current of the oceans and the power of storms. These words rocked me. Just like ice melting against sunlight, all my barriers just vanished with his enlightening words. All the negativities were obliterated in a trice. I was filled with energy and with enthusiasm. My inner world changed completely. I started believing in myself, in the potential that nature has given to all of us. I felt enlightened and awakened.

To me, Sukhvinder, it felt like a revelation, a mental metamorphosis. It affected everything within me, including my gloomy and depressing outlook on life. I felt confident, and was filled with faith and courage. For me, everything that appeared to be difficult turned out to be quite simple and easy. Earlier, I was like an extinguished candle, but it was suddenly lit by the enlightening words of the ascetic. My dream of becoming a millionaire seemed like fetching a drop of water from the ocean now. I was blessed with a positive mindset, filled with a new stream of energy and exuberance. I was endowed with a cheerful outlook and a fresh burst of enthusiasm and vitality."

Well after hearing from Rahul, I became more inquisitive, to know what happened afterwards.

I asked Rahul, "Can you share with me how did you earn all the wealth, did a miracle happen?"

"Sukhvinder, no miracle happened in my life," Rahul remarked with a smile. "It's not like I won a lottery; everything that occurred, happened quite organically. The only change was in my mindset, which was on the right track. Like a bullet train which has derailed and gets stuck in the mud and cannot be moved, but once it is on the rails, it moves at the speed of light, so was my state. My mindset came on the right track and now started running like a bullet train. Those barriers that restricted me every day and every moment were now replaced with tremendous motivation and momentum. There was a great deal of fervor and fire, and I was committed to achieve my goals regardless of the challenges or the circumstances I would face."

I was becoming more desperate to listen to Rahul and know exactly what happened that made him so rich.

Rahul continued, "Sukhvinder, it isn't that the ascetic granted me a prospective opportunity that quickly made me wealthy. Nothing of that happened. My life was pretty hard and I was indeed struggling in the same manner as before. My outer circumstances were the same. Nothing outside of me altered to my advantage."

He continued with his story which was very interesting.

Rahul said, "As I told you, my circumstances were still as before. So, I kept trying for jobs and gave interviews, but no one offered me a good job. My lack of education and skills caused me to fail every interview. I also tried to figure out some business opportunities, but nothing worked out.

Finally, I took a small job as a delivery boy in a courier company and similar other jobs later on. In the evening, sometimes I used to sell some snacks on the footpath, as my income was not sufficient for the survival of my family. I was hardly able to make both ends meet.

For 3 years, I kept struggling. The last job I did was installing cables for a contractor who was working for an electric power generation company. Unfortunately, one day, while repairing an overhead cable, I fell from the ladder and broke my arm. I got a fracture in my arm, and I could not work for two months. The contractor gave me no medical compensation, no salary, and, worst of all, they sacked me as the accident left me incapacitated for several weeks. I recovered after two months. Again, I was jobless and penniless. Whatever small amount I had saved, all went into my medical treatment. I was totally broke at this time.

After this event, I was really disturbed, but I remembered the ascetic words, "Stay positive and stay determined; work hard; and whatever challenges may befall you, don't quit; don't even think to give up. Be persistent and consistent, and stay committed to your goals." His words always resonated in my mind.

I always remained positive. I remained steadfast. I was resolute in my determination to accomplish my goals, undeterred by any challenges that may appear. Though my arm was broken, but my spirit to win was untouched; my financial condition was miserable, but my mental condition was bright; my external circumstances were hopeless, but my internal aspirations were positive. I fell from the ladder, but I didn't fall in my life.

As I would recollect his words, they would put all the energy and zeal within me once again.

However, I was wandering for months here and there and looking for a job. My friends laughed at me at my back, and my relatives said that due to my fate, I will always remain poor and deprived. My condition was even more hopeless than before.

Coincidentally, there was an event in our city—a mega musical concert. The organizer wanted some people on a temporary basis, and through some contacts, I got the job. I was basically an executive who was responsible for supervising a small part of that event. It was hardly a fifteen-day job, and the remuneration was not very good. But I had no choice. I was like a beggar at that time, and as the saying goes, "Beggars have no choices," so was my plight.

Being in a hopeless situation, I took that opportunity positively. I did all the work with all my enthusiasm and zeal. I did my job sincerely. Whatever they instructed, I did with all my heart and soul. Eventually, they liked my work. After the event was over, they offered me a permanent job, as they were looking for young, energetic people.

This company was an event management company. They were organizing all events like mega musical concerts, industrial trade fairs and exhibitions, corporate award functions, health care events, fashion shows, product launch and promotion events, religious events, political events, gala dinners, advertising, etc.

I took that job. The job was very demanding and laborious, and the company exploited me. However, as the ascetic said, work hard, put all your heart and soul into your work, and do it sincerely and honestly. I did exactly what he said. I followed his words religiously.

Within one year, I became the manager. All the major work was under my supervision. Right from organizing the stage, the music system, the lights, the decoration, the security, the advertisement banners, the sitting arrangement, and the parking area, everything was under my supervision. The work was so demanding that sometimes I used to sleep in the event area and was unable to go home. Sometimes, I had to work almost 16 hours a day. During my regular days, I worked for almost 12 hours a day. I never took any leave.

I recall one occasion. June 16th was the date. The company had organized an event in some other city. So, I was out for one week. In the evening, I was entering my date of birth on an authorization form for my name When I was writing the date of birth, I remembered it was June 16th. That day was my birthday. I totally forgot my birthday. At that moment, I realized how alone I am due to my struggles.

Sukhvinder, life was filled with hardships and struggles, nothing more. I felt completely disconnected from everything in my life because of my financial hardships. Day and night, I was just toiling. There were no cell phones in those bygone days. My parents, especially my mother, would have been eager to wish me and bless me, but there were no means that I could contact her or they could contact me.

However, I continued to work with all my heart and soul.

I worked for five years. Because of my hard work, my friendly nature and a helping attitude, I made a lot of friends. All the clients and vendors, including the stage decorator, music system company, light suppliers, security company, and managers of the celebrities, became my best friends. They all knew I was the one who used to put in all the efforts to make the events successful.

My work was the best, but my salary wasn't good. The company exploited me. During the event in other cities, we were not given proper accommodations. Our perks were subpar. The company did not pay any heed to my grievances. However, I had no choice but to continue with my job. Despite the low salary and the exploitation, I worked very hard. Within those five years, I became a master of my work. I had the skills to effectively coordinate and manage events of various scales, from small to large-scale functions. I had comprehensive knowledge of every minute detail and was capable of independently handling all the tasks. I achieved a high level of expertise in my field.

Well, lastly, when I received my increment, it was very disappointing. Consequently, I submitted a formal request to the management, urging them to reassess my salary raise. Unfortunately, they bluntly denied it without acknowledging my hard work and sincere efforts. However, that was a turning point. I could no longer continue with them. So, I thought of starting my own business. Finally, I quit the job and started my own company. I had no money, but I had contacts, and I had made a good reputation with all the clients and vendors. They trusted me. They were ready to support me. They had confidence in me, in my ability, and in my hard work. So, I started my own company. My only strength was my contacts with the clients and suppliers and their trust in my capabilities.

Initially, I planned to organize small events due to my financial constraints. Because of my good contacts, I got the contracts very easily. I organized the events and made all the events successful. I delivered more than the expectations of my clients.

Basically, the company in which I worked had a major problem. The large corporation essentially outsourced nearly all of its work to its suppliers. They were doing nothing on their own except managing. But unfortunately, they gave their contracts at a very low price; secondly, they made the payments very late, and they used to deduct some money, finding unnecessary faults. In other words, they weren't good paymasters. I decided to make their weakness my strength. I decided to pay fairly to my suppliers and make the payments on time. Because of this strategy, my relationships with my suppliers were extremely good.

In the first year, I organized more than 30 events and made a good amount of money. Now I had the financial capability to organize bigger events. I had a big team. I started organizing large-scale events, and money started coming in abundance. From the money I earned, I started making assets. I refrained from incurring any superfluous expenditures. At first, I leased an office space, but as my income increased, I bought my own office. I purchased all the necessary equipment to increase my profit margins. In a span of three years, I purchased a small piece of land on the outskirts where small parties could be organized. I subsequently bought the nearby property and built a modest function hall, then some rooms for accommodation, and I continued growing my business.

As my income increased, I acquired knowledge in construction and eventually started working in real estate. Initially, I did small projects in partnership, and later, I had my own projects. Initially, the projects were of a smaller scale, but as I gained more knowledge, I executed bigger projects. I included my two brothers in my business.

Sukhvinder within 6 to 7 years, my wealth skyrocketed. Finally, I became a multi-millionaire. Now my real estate business is hundred times bigger than my event organizing business. My business is growing, and I am making more investments day by day. There is no end to my wealth now.

As the ascetic said, "Rs. 15 crore is just like fetching a drop of water from the oceans. He was so true. The power that nature has given to us is limitless. No human being is an ordinary being. However, the fortunate realize this fact, and the unfortunate remains ignorant. This is the truth of life and my complete story, Sukhvinder."

I was deeply inspired to listen to Rahul. I was extremely motivated. He did it, and he proved it. A person from zero to a real hero in his life.

Finally, I asked him, "Rahul, how would you like to summarize the key points that contributed to your journey of success?"

He immediately replied, "Sukhvinder, the first thing that helped me was the ascetic's words. Those words made my mindset very positive, and despite the failures and challenges that I encountered at every level, I remained steadfast. I always remained motivated; I was always determined, just because those words resonated in my mind.

No matter how negative the circumstances were, my mindset was always encouraging. I pursued my goals persistently and consistently.

So, the first thing is having a positive mindset. Without your mental strength, you will be totally worthless in life. However, after a good mindset, you need the following:

1. High Energy level.

2. Whatever you do, give your best, do it whole heartedly.

3. Work ethically in life, you can work longer and you will have more supporters to work with you.

4. Don't compromise in the quality of your work.

5. Be positive and think big in life.

Follow the above principles, and believe me, in whatever field you are working, you will be the epitome of success."

It was late at night at Rahul's house, discussing all about success and failure.

It was a memorable and inspiring meeting. It was indeed enlightening to meet Rahul and learn about his successful journey. A person who was uneducated, poor, and incapable, whose life was totally hopeless, created a fortune on his own. His story is a story of dynamism; it's an evolving journey of resilience, ingenuity, and a steadfast commitment to succeed and grow.

As we parted, a profound sense of clarity washed over me. Rahul's story was not just his own; it is a universal narrative of how, just by changing one's mindset, the entire world changes, unlocking doors to unforeseen financial opportunities. It was just like transmuting iron into gold. His story is a magnificent example of the magnitude of a human's willpower, climbing from the depths of poverty to the pinnacles of opulence.

Dear reader, as I, Sukhvinder Singh, recount this anecdote to you, I promise a treasure trove of wisdom within these pages. This book is your guide to elevate your financial destiny to a level you never expected before.

So, the most important point I learned from Rahul was to first throw out all the barriers from our minds that restrict our growth. Basically, we need to make our minds like a fertile land where seeds of success can grow. Often, to think of success is more difficult than to be really successful. Most people gave up not because success was difficult but because they thought so. They had preconceived notions that earning a lot of money was too difficult. That is why they remained poor throughout their lives. It was the poverty in their minds that stuck them in poverty, not the circumstances. So, first, start believing that you can do it.

When we shift from a scarcity mindset to one of abundance, we open ourselves to opportunities, prosperity and success. Wealth, then, becomes not an elusive treasure guarded by the few but a horizon that expands as we approach it.

A million dollars must first be deposited in your head before it arrives in your bank account. Nobody will give you a pay check in your hand until your mind is determined to make it happen.

> **"Once you make a decision,**
> **the universe conspires to make it happen"**
>
> *– Ralph Waldo Emerson.*

The other problem is that most of the time, when we think of achieving our goals, we don't have any clue of how to move towards them; we don't have the resources, direction, or support. So, the question arises, "How will it happen?" This is the most obvious question, which generally comes to everyone.

To understand the phenomenon of how things will happen in our favor, we need to understand the laws of the universe. How to manifest our dreams into reality. One small example would probably clarify your confusion.

To plant a big mango tree, what do we do? Do we go to the store and get such a massive mango tree to plant? No, we take a tiny seed and plant it in the ground. Every day we put in some water and occasionally some manure for its growth, and then we allow nature to take its course. Our contribution is negligible; it is our motherland and nature that does everything. When they are tiny, we shield them from animals and harsh weather. Our contribution to the growth of the tree is that we have sown the seed, put some water in it, taken care of it, and protected it. The fruits appear on their own when they do. We have not added any color, taste, sugar, or nutrients to the fruit. Nature provides everything in the fruit.

Similarly, to make your dreams come true, plant the seed of your dream in your mind. Our mind is the land that will germinate the seed with the help of the universe. The human mind is the sole entity that is irrevocably connected with the vast expanse of the universe. Our mind orchestrates the entire cosmos to align with our aspirations and dreams. Our Universe conspires to support those who embraces life with faith, courage and determination. All we need to do is implant the seed in our mind and nourish it with our unwavering confidence. Just as a diligent gardener works to make a verdant and blooming garden, so must we nurture our mind with the seeds of our dreams and cultivate abundance in our lives. We should plant seeds with positivity, irrigate with confidence, and weed out the choking tendrils of scarcity and doubt. Ponder positive thoughts deeply, for it is the process from which the tree of abundance grows. Tend to this garden, and you shall reap a harvest more bountiful than you ever imagined.

Don't doubt your success. Have confidence in your ability to succeed. Doubt is a formidable force that consumes your achievements. Safeguard your ambitions against doubts. Have unwavering faith in your ability to succeed. Visualize your dreams and objectives daily, and infuse them with unwavering confidence to manifest them into reality.

The universe, along with the power of your subconscious mind, will eventually make it happen. Take every step with faith, and trust that the universe conspires to support those who embrace the fullness of life.

Whatever efforts, contributions, or hard work are required, the universe will take it from us, provided we are committed and sincere in giving our best. We should be prepared and willing to give our small but consistent and unwavering contribution. Eventually, everything will happen on its own. At first, progress may appear to be sluggish, but eventually you will witness the gradual manifestation of your dreams, and as you continue to advance, you will witness the transformation of your dreams into tangible reality.

Imagine if Bill Gates went and sold his software to every individual person in this world. Arnold Schwarzenegger had no background in acting, but he became one of the most popular superstars in Hollywood. Does the owner of McDonald's go house to house to sell his burgers? No, but it still happened. There is some power in making all this happen. It is the power of the universe. All the power of the universe lies within your mind. It all depends on how you harness this power.

I would like to share one more example to enlighten my readers on this topic.

As far as the growth of our body is concerned, what is our contribution? Starting from the body, which took shape in the mother's womb, how did the microscopic cells know about our various body organs like eyes, ears, face, stomach, lever, heart, brain, legs, hands, kidneys, skin, muscles, bones, hair, tongue, nails, fingers, etc.? The complete human body, which is so complicated in its structure and beyond the comprehension of science, is created within nine months without support from any external means.

After the birth of the child, it breathes automatically. The heart functions on its own. The mother only provides milk to the infant. As we grow up, we just eat, drink, and sleep.

The activities that are functioning in our body are infinite and unconceivable. Till today, science does not know how our body makes blood from our food. We eat, and what we eat gets transformed into different parts of our body. This body is self-healing. This body can re-produce. There is not only one activity, but millions going on continuously within our body. How does it happen? Who makes all this happen?

The answer is simple: "It is the universe making all this happen." As long as your direction in life is correct, the universe has been designed to provide all support and care. Unfortunately, people who are deprived of this fact remain ignorant, and they grieve for their failures and circumstances. But successful people know this fact, and despite their limitations, they overcome them with their determination and faith in the power of the universe, which is residing within them.

Most wealthy people were not born rich. Some of them either lived on the streets, in tents, or as orphans; some did not have the privilege of love from their parents or any resources to support them in the journey of their success. However, they succeeded in their profession and took their lives from rags to riches, which they achieved through their positive mindset combined with their hard work and their strong determination.

Charlie Chaplin's journey from poverty to wealth is the most dramatic rags-to-riches tale ever recorded. He was raised without a father, and his mother struggled financially. He supported himself and his brother while earning a little wage. When Chaplin was seven years old, his family put him to Lambeth Workhouse. Chaplin recalled his time as a pauper at the Central London District School being housed by the council as "a forlorn existence." Before turning nine, he had already been taken to a workhouse twice. His mother was admitted to a mental institution when he was fourteen. Charlie Chaplin had a difficult and terrible upbringing, but despite all the challenges and struggles, he became the finest performer of the silent period. His life story became the most tragic Rags to Riches tale ever because of the manner he endured the most unfathomable adversities.

Countless stories exist of individuals who, against all odds, achieved remarkable financial turnarounds by shifting their mindset. These narratives serve not only as inspiration but as concrete examples of the principle in action.

Actual success stories have always started from rags to riches, weaknesses to strength, and failure to achievements.

The first thing is to have confidence in yourself and take the initiative. Make a start at whatever level you can, and then keep moving persistently. If you have strong determination and faith in your success, nothing can stop you.

For people who turned the impossible into possible, the first thing they had was a strong determination. All qualities like positive attitude, commitment, courage, determination, hard work, faith, discipline, etc. are the keys to open the vast energy reservoirs of this universe for the accomplishment of your goals. Use your keys, and you can unlock all the secrets and powers that the universe has given you in abundance to make you successful.

Take out your mental block that I am poor and I cannot become rich. Feed your mind with positive thinking, start working hard with faith and determination, and gradually you will find your milestones getting achieved, like a miracle. Your mind will finally become the boat, ready to embark on the journey, teeming with opportunities, provided you have the will to sail and face the challenges with courage and conviction.

In conclusion, the journey to financial success is as much about unlearning as it is about learning. It involves dismantling the limiting beliefs that hold us back and constructing a new set of empowering convictions. Examine the beliefs that constrain your financial prosperity. Challenge them. Replace them with convictions that empower you.

Overcome your mental block that whispers "I am poor" and replace it with the one saying loudly that "**I am Rich,**" "**I am Rich,**" and "**I am Rich.**"

IS SUCCESS BY LUCK OR BY MERITS?

Whenever we talk about success, a lot of people believe that success is based on luck and not merits. It's a concept that evokes debate, divides opinions, and has been a subject of deep contemplation. What is luck? Can it be captured, harnessed, or is it a fleeting wisp, always just beyond our grasp?

Before we examine whether success is by merits or luck, let me share with you a little story.

There was a giant lottery firm with a staggering jackpot of "**One billion US dollars**." They operated on a grand scale. Millions of people used to purchase tickets, but according to the rules, there was only one winner in every drawing, which happened once a year. When the deadline arrived, the winner was announced.

Charlie was the winner's name. Charlie was sadly not there that day, but his buddy John, who was in possession of the ticket, attended on his behalf. But according to the rules, only the winner would receive the cheque in person. John was thus unable to take the reward. However, John informed that since Charlie was not expecting to win, he did not come, but he could come the other day to collect the cheque.

The corporation had no issues because the winner had seven days leeway to pick up the cheque.

Once again, the event was organized. Thousands of people came the other day when Charlie was due to get the lottery money. Everyone was eager to witness one of the world's luckiest men. It was really an exciting occasion. However, the moment Charlie appeared on the stage, everyone was shocked to see him. Basically, Charlie was not a human being but a donkey. His owner has taken the lottery in his name, and by luck, the donkey named Charlie won one billion dollars. The moral of the story is:

"What is the pride in winning a race
where even a Donkey can win."

I hope the message is very clear. If someone wins a billion dollars through a lottery or luck, it is not a meaningful success.

The first thing we need to understand is that success is never by luck. If anything is achieved by luck, without merits, it will be meaningless and short-lived.

Hence, the foundation of success is always merits.

Now, further analysis is needed to determine if people are lucky then what happens in the long run.

There is a small analytical example that would clarify how much luck or merits contributes to your success.

Once, a multinational company gave its distributorship to two people. One was Tom, and another was John.

Tom is the lucky fellow, and John is like a common man. Except for luck, both persons have the same product, the same price, and the same market potential. On average, the hit ratio was 20% in the business. However, since Tom was lucky, his ratio was 60% and John's hit ratio was 20%, just average. Hence, Tom visited three clients every day and used to get two orders, since he was lucky. John visited 10 clients and used to get 2 orders since he was not as lucky as Tom. Hence, he had to work harder to meet the targets of the company. After one year, the statistics of the business of Tom and John were as follows:

	First Year	
	Clients visited	**Orders received**
Tom (Lucky)	750	450
John (Unlucky)	2000	400

As per the above table, you can see that Tom visited 750 clients in the first year and got 450 orders, whereas John visited 2000 clients and got 400 orders. The difference in the final outcome was not very significant, but John had to work pretty hard.

Now, after one more year, i.e., they both continued to work in the same way. As you are aware, the problem with luck is that it does not favour everyone every time, so in the second year, luck was with no one, neither Tom nor John. They were on their own. Hence, the results after 2 years, based on an average hit ratio of 20%, were as follows:

	First Year		Second Year		Order from previous clients of first year	Total orders for second year	Total order for first and second year	Total number of clients
	Clients visited	Orders received	Clients visited	Orders received				
		a		b	c	b+c	a+b+c	
Tom	750	450	750	150	60 from 300 taking 20% ratio / 300 x 20% = 60	150+60 = 210	450+210 = 660	1500
John	2000	400	2000	400	1600 x 20% = 320	400 + 320 = 720	400+720= 1120.	4000

Tom visited 750 clients in the next year and got 150 (20%) orders, plus 60 orders from the visits made in the previous year. Total orders for Tom are 660 cumulative for the first and second years.

Regarding John, he visited 2000 clients and obtained 400 orders (20%), in addition to 320 orders from previous visits. Therefore, there were a combined total of 1120 orders during the course of the first and second years.

Finally, John had covered more market areas, gained more experience, cultivated a larger clientele, established a substantial network, and had a better understanding of business. Hence, John's business was growing by leaps and bounds, whereas Tom's business was very low compared to John's. Within the next few years, Tom did not do very well because luck does not favor everyone every time. By the time Tom realized this fact, it was too late because he was dependent on luck, which did not support him in the subsequent years. Also, Tom had become lazy, ineffective, and demotivated as he could not work hard and finally, he failed.

The moral of the story is that luck failed Tom, and hard work made John successful in the long run. Do not pray to God to give you success by luck, but pray to God to give you the ability and merits that make you strong and capable.

If you want to build a nice house, it is imperative that the four pillars of the house have to be strong. If your structural engineer tells you, "Out of four, only three pillars are strong, whereas the fourth is relatively weak because I have left that pillar to the mercy of your luck, what would you say?"

If a doctor tells you that he will do only half the operation and the rest will be left to the patient's luck, what would you say?

If the airline says that their pilot will fly the plane half way and the other half will be left to your luck, will you fly in that airplane?

Can you imagine how absurd it would be if the instructor at the school told you that they would only teach half of the curriculum and that the remaining half would rely on the pupils' luck?

But we do the same in our lives. Consider the scenario when we base our plans for success on luck. Relying on luck as the foundation for our success is absurd.

We need to check: did we do all our work thoroughly? did we fly with our full wings open? did we run with all our energy? and did we work with all our heart and soul?

How many things have we taken charge of responsibly and sincerely, and how much have we left to luck? Upon careful examination we would discover that almost everything has been handed over to luck and when we fail, we start blaming our fate, our family, our circumstances, etc.

Attaining success by luck is like engaging in gambling. The most ambiguous entity. However, we still want to play this game, and we risk losing it every time.

Hence, I would like to specifically mention here that for strong stability in life, we need to cross the barriers of bad luck and good luck and reach a level where success is not at the caprices of our luck but on the strength of our ability and merits. This is what meaningful success is.

In truth, the journey to wealth is often a marathon, not a sprint. It demands discipline, strategic planning, and, crucially, a tolerance for risk and failure. The rare stories of instantaneous wealth capture our imagination precisely because they are exceptions, not the rule. To dispel this myth, we must embrace the reality that wealth is typically the result of enduring effort and smart, sustained strategies.

As we journey through the forest of financial myths, we must arm ourselves with knowledge, diligence, and a discerning eye. Wealth is not the result of shortcuts or mere circumstance; it is cultivated through a combination of hard work, strategic decision-making, and a deep understanding of the principles of money management.

Going a step further, I would like to state that you must elevate yourself to such a level that others perceive it as luck to be associated with you.

For instance, an individual who secures employment with prestigious firms like Mercedes, BMW, Boeing, Airbus, Google, NASA, and similar establishments would perceive himself as lucky. Students who get admitted to the University of Oxford or Harvard University consider themselves lucky. These institutes and organizations have elevated themselves to such a level that people consider themselves lucky to associate with or be a part of them. Why not take ourselves to such a level in life that people would consider themselves lucky to associate with us? Just think!!!

All said and done, in the long run, people depending on luck will ultimately experience a dismal failure, whereas people who have worked hard and are sincere will grow and succeed during all the phases of their lives.

Consider a scenario where a gambler is seated at a roulette table, and at every spin expects to win, despite the low probability. Now picture a businessman who purchased a plot of land with the vision that it would become the prime location during the development of the city in near future. After a few years of city development, his land becomes highly desirable and its value increases significantly.

Considering the above examples, both are at the mercy of chance, yet the businessman's luck is cultivated through knowledge, strategy, and vision. This allegory illustrates a profound truth: while we cannot control luck, we can position ourselves to capitalize on it when it strikes.

In the words of the wise Seneca, "Luck is what happens when preparation meets opportunity." Let us then prepare, so that when opportunity knocks, luck will find us ready to answer the call.

In summary, harnessing luck for financial prosperity is not about waiting for stars to align but about preparing ourselves to the impending opportunities that seeks the deserving. It is a blend of skills, hard work, patience, discipline, commitment, courage etc all converging to create a magnet for opportunity which eventually pays you in abundance.

HOW TO EARN MONEY
AND THEN MORE MONEY

When I was young, I started my own business. I was energetic, educated, and honest. Despite my diligent and persistent efforts over a period of 5 years, I ultimately experienced failure. I became broke. Having no options left, I took a job. But following this encounter, I was left with an intriguing question that bothered me for a long time. The question was, "Why didn't I earn money?"

Why didn't I earn money?

I was educated, honest, enthusiastic, hardworking and still I didn't earn money? I was extremely curios to know the answer. I wanted to know from where does money come precisely? It seemed as if my understanding regarding money was not clear. I need to learn more. I need to know the fundamentals.

Like a common man we pretend to know a lot about today's world, but we don't know precisely about anything. In this fast-moving world, where communication and information are moving at the speed of light, all knowledge is superficial and shallow. It has lost precision and depth. So was the case with my knowledge pertaining to money. I thought I knew, but actually I didn't know. I accepted the fact that my knowledge about money is absolutely nil and that I am totally ignorant. Hence, my journey started. My journey began with a desire to learn the fundamentals and intricacies of money.

I wanted to know the answer to my question "Why didn't I earn money?" I also wanted to know from where does money come, precisely and exactly.

Hence, I started meeting a lot of people, mainly the rich, and I asked them the basic thing, which was, "From where does money come?"

They all gave me various answers, which were mostly absurd, and I was left totally unassuaged.

Some told me that I needed to work hard, which I did. Some told me to work smart, and when I asked them what smart work is, they all gave me vague answers. However, most people told me that money always comes from money or that money makes money, which, according to me, was incorrect.

Nevertheless, this fallacy is very popular, and people strongly believe that money makes money.

This great paradox has plagued countless souls: To make money, one must have money. This is the conundrum in which we find ourselves entangled, and it is as ubiquitous as it is profound. So let us untie this Gordian knot, which has confined the mindset of millions and deprived them of the ability to move ahead.

If money makes money, then why did all the big companies that were the largest in the world, at some point, failed and became broke within a few years?

If money makes money, then why have so many banks gone bankrupt?

First Republic Bank, a San Francisco-based regional bank with assets over \$200 billion, closed on May 1st, 2023. It was a third major U.S. bank. Why money didn't make money in this case?

Similarly, Silicon Valley Bank (SVB), the 16th largest bank in the United States, closed down on March 10th, 2023. The bank had assets of about \$209 billion in December 2022.

Why money didn't make money in this instance?

Bank failures like this have happened so many times. More than 550 banks shut down from 2001 to 2023, according to the Federal Deposit Insurance Corp. (FDIC).

As per the research of the Harvard Business Review, it reveals that since 2000, 52% of companies in the Fortune 500 list have either gone bankrupt, been acquired, or ceased to exist.

Similarly, I could list hundreds more instances of billion-dollar corporations that went completely bankrupt in a matter of years. If money makes money, why did their money fail to do so?

The truth is, money never makes money. However, this saying is good to sympathize with and cajole poor people. They always live under the misconception that their poverty is solely due to lack of money. However, if we want to be rich, it is imperative that we come out of this fallacy.

Further, someone told me money comes after experience. Well again that was not very true. Bill Gates had no experience about business still he became the richest man on earth. So was Steve jobs. So, people advices were incorrect.

Having no choice, I stopped discussing with people and started reading books to have a precise answer. I read a lot of books, articles and theories on money but I did not get the precise answer to what I was looking for. However, books enhanced my reasoning, my creativity, they advanced my thinking and they provoked me to explore more on this subject and eventually get the right answer. Finally, after three years of consistent reading about money, I got the precise answer. I would like to share with you the answer in a one-line morsel of wisdom as follows:

"Money comes only from one quality and that is "Skills."

The above is a universal truth. Money only follows skills in this world. I shall provide various examples, in support to this. I shall share with you a remarkable incident that how skills make money rather than money making money.

In August 1972, Idi Amin, the President of Uganda, issued a directive mandating the expulsion of the Asian population in his country, granting them a period of 90 days to depart from the nation. During the deportation, there were an estimated 60,000-80,000 persons of Indian heritage residing in Uganda. The expulsion occurred because of racial discrimination, resulting into anti-Indian sentiment. The exiled Asians were industrious individuals with exceptional entrepreneurial skills, adept in commerce, and they were the fundamental support of the economy. Nevertheless, Idi Amin proceeded to forcibly remove them, thereafter transferring their assets and enterprises to his associates, who rapidly squandered them due to their incompetence and mismanagement.

All the property of the Asians, their farms, factories, houses, ranches, estates etc were confiscated, along with cars, homes and other household goods.

Asians who were expelled had the option to leave with just $120 in their possession and a limit of 485 lbs. of personal belongings. As per some reports even the ornaments of the Indian ladies were confiscated at the Uganda Airport. The Asians left the country with their homes open, and they even left the cars with their keys inside. It was a devastating situation for them.

At the time of their deportation, Indians owned 90% of the country's businesses and contributed 90% of Uganda's tax income.

Nevertheless, shortly after the expulsion, the economy of Uganda saw a decline.

Several Asian firms were transferred to Ugandans, who lacked the knowledge and expertise to effectively manage them. One Ugandan individual, who was handed a garments shop, allegedly sold all the items based on the information displayed on the labels, which basically indicated their size and not their price. This ultimately resulted in a complete financial loss.

Likewise, the new Ugandan owners of the country's cement factory in Tororo failed to recognize the necessity of regularly cleaning the facility's roof. Consequently, the accumulation of cement dust led to the collapse of the roof.

Hence, transferring ownership of these enterprises to indigenous Ugandans proved ineffective as most lacked the skills to run them. The industrial sector in Uganda, which was regarded as the fundamental support of the economy, suffered significant harm as a result of a scarcity of skilled labor. The manufacturing production had a significant decline, dropping from 740 million Ugandan shillings in 1972 to 254 million shillings in 1979.

This exemplified the characteristics of everything. Nothing worked after the Asians were expelled.

Paradoxically, the individuals most negatively affected by the expulsion were not the Asians who lost their property, but rather the Ugandan economy, which underwent a rapid decline of 90% in terms of income and earnings within a span of less than ten years.

However, when President Yoweri Museveni seized power in 1986, he encouraged the exiles to return. Museveni condemned Amin's polices and extended an invitation to the Indians to come back.

Thousands of Indians returned to Uganda starting in 1986.

Since their return to the country, Asians from the Indian subcontinent have once again emerged as a crucial support for the nation's economy.

Hence it is not the money, but it is the skills, that attracts money. Despite taking all the money and wealth from the Asians, the country's overall economic condition deteriorated. Contrary to expectations, the people of Uganda did not get wealthier despite the acquisition of all the riches. The nation was severely impacted by poverty and scarcity. This is due to the simple reason that money does not come from money, it comes only from skills.

In the absence of the required skills within an organization, a country, or a family, money will go away in no time.

I would like to share a small story from my book "**Seven Qualities to be Wealthy for Seven Generations**" regarding money and skills.

Once, a Guru was trying to preach the above principle to his disciples, but they didn't take the Guru's advice seriously.

One day, he gathered all his students and gave them a small box made up of clay. He asked them to go to the market and sell it and get a good deal. All the students wandered in the market throughout the day, trying to sell the box, but were unsuccessful. They came back in the evening to the monastery.

The Guru asked what happened, and the students replied, "No one bought the box."

The Guru said, "Fine, no problem."

The next day, the Guru came and asked the student, "Make one more attempt to sell the box."

The students, out of reverence, reluctantly acquiesced and went again to the market to sell the box of clay. They wandered in the market and tried hard for the whole day, but no one bought. They came back tired with the same answer.

The third day, the Guru again approached the students and asked them to try for the last time. The students were quite reluctant, but due to a strong insistence, they agreed.

The students tried hard for the third time, but no one bought that box of clay. This time the situation was awful, as some people laughed at them, some ridiculed them, and asked them to leave and not come again with that cheap box of clay. They were insulted badly by everyone.

Finally, the students returned quite exasperated and disappointed. They told the Guru, "Now people are laughing at us; they have insulted us on seeing this cheap box of clay in our hands. We are totally frustrated, and we will never go to the market again."

The next day, the Guru called his students, gave them the same box of clay, and asked them to go again.

"We will not go to the market to sell this cheap box of clay," the students retorted with brevity.

"Hold on," said the Guru. "Look, I changed something in this box."

"What change?" the students asked curiously.

The Guru said, "I have placed a precious diamond in the box."

He opened the box, and there was a precious sparkling diamond inside. The diamond seemed to be invaluable. On seeing the diamond, the students got excited and agreed to sell the box of clay.

The students went to the market and came back within an hour. They seemed to be happy and joyful. They managed to sell the box at a good price.

They said to the Guru, "Finally, we have sold your box of clay at a very good price."

The Guru asked, "Excellent! But how did you manage to sell the box this time?"

The students responded, "We went to the market. We opened the box and showed the diamond to the buyers. On seeing the diamond, a lot of buyers got interested. Within no time, the auction started, and within 10 minutes, we secured the best deal."

The Guru remarked, "Great. You have done a good job today. Nevertheless, what insights have you gained and learned from this particular experience?"

The students exclaimed in astonishment, "Learned!!! What do you mean by saying that? What did we learn from this experience? There is nothing to learn. You gave us a box of clay with a diamond in it to sell in the market. We followed your recommendations and sold the clay box. What more is there to learn now?"

"My son, an essential lesson can be gleaned from this incident," the Guru said with a merry smile.

Surprisingly, the students inquired, "What lesson?"

The Guru replied, "We human beings are just like the box of clay. The box of clay holds no intrinsic worth within the context of the business or professional realm. Nevertheless, our skills resemble the precious diamond. Once we possess skills, our worth increases significantly. Individuals in the professional realm will only appreciate you if you possess some valuable skills. Devoid of skills, the professional world will never appreciate your worth; instead, they may belittle or ridicule you. To enhance your value, focus on developing important skills within yourself.

The Guru continued, "In this professional world, the unfortunate truth is that people do not value people. They only value their skills. The true value of people in this materialistic world is the value of their skills. Beggars beg, and they do not get a penny sometimes, whereas skilled people get in abundance before they demand."

The story ends here. The disciples were profoundly moved by the veracity that their Guru imparted.

Dear readers, based on my extensive 28-year tenure in the corporate world, I would like to assert that inside this professional sphere, it is not the person who is valued; it is only the skills. If you don't have valuable skills, the corporate world will regard you as worthless.

I trust that this point is crystal clear.

Further, there is a saying, **"If you took all the money in the world and divided it equally among everybody, it would soon all be back in the same pockets."**

The question is to which pockets the money would go back. The answer is that it would go to those pockets where there are skills.

In addition, according to a study by the Georgetown University Centre on Education and the Workforce, the lifetime earnings of those with a bachelor's degree are 84% greater than those with only a high school diploma. Upon closer inspection, these figures appear to be exclusively pertaining to wages; however, upon further analysis, they also reveal information regarding individual empowerment, career progression, and job satisfaction.

Money comes solely from abilities; everything else holds no worth in our materialistic world. Investing in your own skill set is the most profitable venture you will ever undertake. Each new skill mastered opens doors that were previously invisible, expands your horizons, and yields fairly good returns, not just in monetary terms but in personal fulfilment too.

In conclusion, skill acquisition remains a cornerstone of financial success and personal advancement. The skills you acquire are a bridge to opportunities and a testament to the enduring power of financial prosperity.

I hope this point is clear. Now I would like to go to the next point. Skills will get you money, but skills do not get you a lot of money. So, the question is how to earn a lot of money. Let's now go to the next level. How to earn a substantial amount of money or more money.

Everyone is getting in commensurate with one's skills. An engineer, a doctor, a lawyer, a businessman, a professional. Money is directly proportional to your skills. However, skills will get you average money. But if you intend to earn a lot of money or become a millionaire or a billionaire, then one needs to have exceptional skills, what we call as **"EXPERTISE."**

Expertise is the only quality that will get you colossal amount of money. All those people who are multimillionaires are basically experts in their field. Regardless of the discipline to which they belong, they are all experts.

Just imagine the fees of a renowned surgeon, an expert lawyer, Information Technology specialists, Artificial Intelligence (AI) Engineers, Aerospace engineers etc. Money flows in abundance to such experts.

There is only one quality that generates substantial wealth, and that is "**Expertise.**" Irrespective of the domain in which one operates, if he is not an expert, he will not earn colossal money.

Just check on all the millionaires; they are all experts in their field, whether they are businessmen, athletes, Hollywood stars, singers, engineers, lawyers, doctors, motivational speakers, authors, etc.

Without a team of professionals, even an ambitious entrepreneur would struggle to achieve business growth. For a successful business, it is important to have a team of experts. Through experts only, one can manage to achieve great heights, effectively and efficiently, and maintain stability in business.

Without expertise, it is not possible to make yourself eligible to become a millionaire or a billionaire. Let us now gain a deeper understanding of experts.

Qualities of Experts:

- Experts know their work better than anyone else.

- The world follows the experts only.

- Experts don't create a network; they are followed by a great number of people.

- People trust the experts and follow them unconditionally.

- People want to be guided by experts and take motivation from them.

- Experts are less in number and more in demand.

- Money, fame, and opportunity follow the experts.

- Entrepreneurs put all their money on experts.

- Expertise reduces the risk of failure.

- Expertise confers security, stability, and expansion in its respective domain.

- Experts are usually known as "God fathers."

The world is a fervent seeker of experts.

Hence, if we want to earn more money, the only channel is "Expertise." Money comes in abundance through the channel of expertise.

Let me share more details with you, considering the statistics pertaining to money and expertise.

One important thing we need to understand about money is that money does not come to anyone by causal means. Money strictly remains in the quadrant of people with skills and expertise. The content on the following pages would help to provide a clear understanding of this subject.

Table 1: Global Household Wealth distribution pattern.

Year	Top 1%	Top 5%	Top 10%	Bottom 90%
2010	43.6	70.2	82.8	17.2
2011	44.2	71.6	84.3	15.7
2012	45.75	73.58	85.62	14.38
2013	46.35	73.97	85.95	14.05
2014	48.15	75.68	87.38	12.62
2015	50.01	76.6	87.65	12.35

Year	Top 1%	Top 5%	Top 10%	Bottom 90%
2016	50.8	77.69	89.1	10.9
2017	50.13	76.44	87.82	12.18
2018	47.2	73.4	84.8	15.2
2019	45	70.2	81.7	18.3
2020	43.2	71	81.8	18.2
2021	44.9	70.1	81.8	18.2
2022	45.6	70.4	81.9	18.1

Source : Credit Suisse report.

From the above table, it is evident that the maximum wealth in the world lies with only 1% of the top-class people. These are the people who are exceptional in their field. Similarly, the top 10% of the population holds almost 80% of the world's wealth, and the rest bottom 90% of people have only 12% to 18% wealth.

Further, I have studied the wealth pattern of U.S.A. The below table shows the share of wealth by the top 1%, top 20%, and bottom 80% in the United States from year 1962 to year 2016.

Distribution of Net worth and financial wealth in the United State 1962–2016.

Table 2

Year	Top 1.00%	Top 20.00%	Bottom 80.00%
1962	33.4%	81.0%	19.0%
1969	35.6%	82.5%	17.5%
1983	33.8%	81.3%	18.7%
1989	35.2%	83.0%	17.0%
1992	37.2%	83.8%	16.2%
1995	38.5%	83.9%	16.1%
1998	38.1%	83.4%	16.6%

	Top	Top	Bottom
2001	33.4%	84.4%	15.6%
2004	34.3%	84.7%	15.3%
2007	34.6%	85.0%	15.0%
2010	35.1%	88.6%	11.4%
2013	36.7%	88.9%	11.1%
2016	39.6%	89.9%	10.1%

Source: Economist Edward N. Wolff at New York University.

From the above table, the top 1% (**the upper class**) owned 39.6% of all privately held wealth, and the next 19% (**the managerial, professional, and small business stratum**) had 50.3%, which means that just 20% of the people owned a remarkable wealth between 81% to 89.9% of total wealth, leaving only 19% to 10.1% of the wealth for the bottom 80% (wage and salary workers).

Further in those 40 years the wealth of the bottom 80% people has reduced from 19% to 10.1%.

With the above figures, it is very clear that money is exclusively concentrated among individuals possessing exceptional skills and expertise.

From the above tables we can conclude the wealth distribution on global basis on an average as under:

Table-3

Wealth Distribution		
	Quadrant 1	Quadrant 2
Population	Top 10%	Bottom 90%
Wealth	80% to 85%	15% to 20%

Wealth Distribution

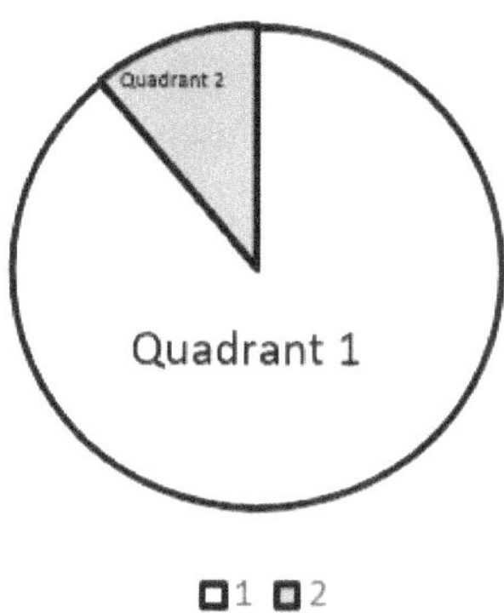

Quadrant 1 : 80-85% wealth with 10% population.

Quadrant 2 : 15-20% wealth with 90% population.

Based on the above data, Quadrant 1, where people with expertise and skills reside, contains the highest amount of wealth, while Quadrant 2, where the common man resides, has a significantly lower amount of wealth.

The most important thing is to observe that money never leaves Quadrant 1. If you look at the history of money in the above tables, you will observe that money has always remained in Quadrant 1.

Let us pause for a moment. If someone asks me to provide the address where money lies in abundance, I would like to give a straight-forward answer. The precise address where money is immensely available is in Quadrant 1.

Money never leaves Quadrant 1, which means if we need to earn more money, we should elevate ourselves and travel to Quadrant 1. Money is not going to come to Quadrant 2. While living in Quadrant 2, don't expect to be rich. If we intend to become richer, then it is imperative that we meet the standards of Quadrant 1, which means we should develop skills and expertise. Without having any special skills, lying in Quadrant 2, no one has ever become rich in the past, and no one will become in the future. If we desire to become a millionaire, we need to elevate ourselves with the help of our skills and expertise so that we can qualify ourselves to the requirements of Quadrant 1.

You can also call Quadrant 1 the treasure island, where money flows in abundance.

If you are within the top 10% of people, you will be rich, and if you are within the top 1%, you will be exceptionally rich. To put it another way, being competent will make you wealthy, but being extraordinarily skilled—that is, being an expert—will make you extremely wealthy. To achieve financial freedom, it is essential to position oneself in Quadrant 1.

Hence, one thing is very clear: what we need to achieve is skills and expertise. In order to truly achieve wealth, it is imperative that we cultivate valuable abilities and subsequently attain mastery in those areas.

During the induction of our new employees, I consistently emphasize to them: "Your objective should not be to attain the highest rank within this organization, but rather to strive for excellence on a global scale. You should achieve such profound expertise in your chosen domain that no one else on earth can match your proficiency."

I would like to emphasize once again to my readers that regardless of the field you choose, your ultimate objective should be to attain global excellence. You ought to possess expertise in your respective domain. If your goal is to accumulate millions of dollars, then you have no alternative. The one recourse remaining is to attain mastery. The immutable reality is that money is unconditionally allocated to the experts and perpetually retained by them.

It is not that poor people are unfortunate, rather, their lack of specialized skills or competence is the primary cause of their poverty.

Hence, the first thing every professional should seek is **"Expertise, Expertise, and Expertise."**

I hope the above is now clear. Let's move further.

Now the question arises as to how one might attain expertise. What specific qualities are required to attain expertise?

In this discussion, I will outline the steps to achieve expertise. I shall delineate the precise qualities required to get mastery. The guidelines that I would be sharing would apply to anyone, irrespective of the field to which they belong. It doesn't matter whether you are a singer, dancer, engineer, doctor, scientist, author, etc., but the below principles would apply to anyone striving to achieve excellence.

The following are the essential attributes needed to attain expertise:

1. Identify your field of interest.

2. Practise.

3. Guidance from experts.

4. Thorough knowledge.

5. Concentration.

It is your skills that get you money, but it is your expertise that gets you more money.

So, to become an expert, the first thing is to know your aptitude, which means identifying the field of your interest. Hence, one must initially ascertain their proclivity by identifying the domain that captivates their interest.

Identify the field of your interest.

The biggest mistake we make in our lives is that we do what other people do, what our father has been doing, or sometimes what my neighbour has been doing. We are good copycats. We want to copy successful people. If you want to become an expert, you should find the field of your own interest.

Nature has made us unique, and hence we are different from others. We are different from others in various aspects of our lives, including our personalities, abilities, skills, experiences, aptitude, emotions, etc. Hence, embracing our uniqueness allows us to fully express ourselves, grow to our maximum potential, and eventually contribute to the diversity of the world around us.

What happened if Michael Jackson, instead of a singer, tried to become a doctor; if Steve Jobs tried to become a singer; if Bill Gates, instead of his passion for computers, tried to pursue and become a professor of biology? These experts did what they loved to do.

Steve Jobs withdrew from college for the simple reason that he did not find the coursework fascinating; furthermore, his lack of interest rendered the education economically unproductive. Steve Jobs mentions in his speech at Stanford that after six months of his joining, he could not see any value, so he dropped out. The best thing, according to him, was that he could stop taking the required classes, which didn't interest him. "It wasn't romantic."

Alternatively, calligraphy lessons at Reed College could be the best in the nation. Having dropped out, Steve had no need to attend the regular class, so he took an interest in calligraphy and chose to learn how to write in it.

According to Steve Jobs' speech, he gained knowledge of "serif and san serif typefaces," how to alter the spacing between distinct letter combinations, and what makes excellent typography exceptional.

"I thought it intriguing because it was elegant, historical, and subtly artistic in a manner that science cannot explain. None of this had even the slightest chance of any practical application in my life," he adds in his address.

"However, it all came back to me 10 years later when we were creating the first Macintosh computer, and we included everything in the Mac's design. The first computer with exquisite typography was this one. The Mac would never have had many typefaces or fonts spaced proportionately if I had never taken that one college course. Furthermore, it's unlikely that any home computer would contain them, given that Windows just copied the Mac. This calligraphy lesson would not have been available to me if I hadn't dropped out, and computers may not have the beautiful typography they do." says Steve.

Hence, find the field that interests you and excel at your skills sincerely. Therefore, identify the area of your passion and diligently master your talents.

The second quality that is important to become an expert is practice.

Practise, Practise and Practise: Practice is crucial, and I am repeating the word "Practice" since it entails consistent and disciplined efforts executed in the correct manner. A musician would practice by repeatedly performing the same exercises; a mathematician would engage in deliberate practice by solving analogous examples; a doctor would practice by repetitively examining comparable case histories within their profession; and a lawyer would practice by repetitively reviewing legislation and analogous case files. Practice is, therefore, just repetition.

Bruce Lee said, "I fear not the man who has practiced 10,000 kicks once, but I fear the man who has practiced one kick 10,000 times".

Practice leads to advancement with every repetition, which eventually fosters progress and improvement. From a technical standpoint, whenever we start practicing, the first stage is being consciously incompetent. For example, when we start learning to ride a bicycle, we are afraid of falling, and we do fall several times. We are consciously incompetent at this stage.

However, after practicing, we eventually gain the ability to balance the bicycle and progressively improve our ability to ride without falling. Hence, the next stage is consciously competent. Now we can ride the bicycle, but we need to be very conscious about our manoeuvring, pushing the paddles, and balancing.

Nevertheless, with continued practice, one attains subconscious competence, which entails peddling the bicycle without consciously engaging with it. We are now capable of riding the bicycle without conscious effort. At this stage, there is no fear of falling, and we can now ride the bicycle without our conscious attention. This stage is subconsciously competent.

The last and fourth level is the level of subconscious proficiency. We can now ride a bicycle without being aware of our movements or balance while our hands are in our pockets. We converse with friends, listen to music, etc. while riding the bicycle. Without our conscious involvement, everything flows organically from our subconscious mind. We refer to this stage as "Expertise."

I am a singer too. I occasionally perform before a sizable congregation. To improve my performance, I practice the hymns I am supposed to sing a day before the event. I keep singing them again and again. I keep practicing for several hours before my performance. With my practice, I get so involved in it, just as sugar dissolves into milk. So does my music, which I want to sing, gets totally dissolved and completely ingrained within me, and then finally, when I sing with such ease and spontaneity that it seems like I'm just breathing. This is the benefit of doing the right kind of practice: it dissolves and integrates the skills into your mind, body, and soul easily. Repetitive practice will enhance your performance to the point where it becomes as natural and effortless as breathing. When you perform, it will come as naturally as your breath. Then it doesn't matter if you are performing in front of a single individual or a large audience. It is inconsequential.

No need to be rigorous but need to be regular: When we are motivated, we feel like touching the sky. At that point, we have all the energy, and we can go to any extreme. At this juncture, people often become very rigorous in their practices. However, this has to be avoided. Reserve your energy and enthusiasm and employ it judiciously with your intellect in a balanced way, so that we do not over practice and cause harm to ourselves. For example, if you want to increase your weight, you cannot do so by eating 10 kg of food in one day. Every day, you have to eat the right kind of nutritious and balanced food. Therefore, to accomplish anything, you must do it consistently and in proper manner, rather than in an extreme manner. This is the law of nature. A tree becomes a tree not within one day but rather spans across several years. Thus, be regular and avoid being rigorous.

Be persistent and consistent: The problem with all of us is that in the beginning, we are quite consistent in all our practices, but later on, we lose our consistency as our motivation goes down. Especially when we hear a motivational lecture, we often experience a surge of inspiration that compels us to promptly engage in work. For a few days, we are regular. However, later on, we become sporadic or we discontinue. This should be avoided.

It is very important to be consistent in our practices, as consistency will bring exponential results. Practicing persistently and consistently multiplies results a million times. Just like the water hitting the rocks consistently, it finally breaks the rock. It is not due to the impact; it is due to the consistency with which the water hits the rock. This is a clandestine principle that all accomplished individuals follow inevitably.

Our subconscious mind is most affected and tuned by anything that is done repeatedly in a consistent way. Any action that we do regularly becomes ingrained in our subconscious minds. In essence, our subconscious mind serves as both a master performer and a keen student. To cultivate our subconscious mind into a proficient learner, we must engage in repetitive actions, thereby fostering its development into masterful performance through a meticulous student.

You can check with any athlete in this world who got their gold medals at the Olympics. The key factor was persistent and consistent practice. Unfortunately, there is no shortcut to this exercise.

Practice with concentration: Without concentration, our practice would be hollow. When I learned classical music from my Guru, one thing he stressed from the beginning was that the foundation of music is based on only one thing, i.e., concentration. In order to improve one's singing ability, one must first develop deep concentration. No person in this world who has poor concentration can become a good singer or a good musician.

"While listening, while practicing, and while singing, you need to focus all your attention, or else it will be just a waste of time coming to my classes, writing notes, etc." he always emphasized.

The renowned Indian Ghazal singer, "Mr. Jagjit Singh," who was my father's good friend, used to visit our home frequently. One day someone at our house was singing, and my father and Jagjit Singh were listening to him. After he finished singing, he told Jagjit Singh that he has been practicing music for the last 15 years, and in a flash, Jagjit Singh replied, "Don't count music into years; if you don't have the right concentration and guidance, your 15 years could be just a waste."

**"Concentration will lead you to depths,
and depths will lead you to heights."**

Examine your level of concentration as you practice. Concentration is a crucial factor that securely embeds your practice in your subconscious mind and strengthens its foundations.

Even after achieving excellence, practicing is important. Skills are not like clothes that you put in your wardrobe and can wear to a party at any time. The moment you do not work on your skills, they start degrading. Hence, practice is inevitable to keep your skills lively at every stage of life.

With all said and done, practice done with concentration, under the right guidance, persistently, and consistently will ultimately result in expertise or excellence. This expertise will lead you to an unparalleled echelon where money, fame, and opportunity will fall on your feet.

Guidance from experts: In order to have faster growth and expertise, it is imperative that we consult and take guidance from the experts. The experts, through their experience and knowledge, will provide the right guidance and help us to desist from doing what is unnecessary. Doing something on our own can lead to mistakes, may take more time, and may lead to imperfections, confusions, and complications. However, the privilege of proper guidance will give you clarity, give you the right sequence of doing things in a proper manner, help you avoid making mistakes and wasting time on unnecessary things. Eventually, it will give you a shorter, smarter, more efficient, and more effective way to reach targeted outcomes.

Whatever we do in our lives, we have to do it the right way.

Only an expert can create another expert. Without consulting an expert, the journey would be long, protracted, perplexing, and complicated. Hence, take guidance from experts.

Thorough knowledge: In today's world, most of the problems persist just because people do not have thorough knowledge. A significant number of issues endure due to individuals lacking comprehensive knowledge. Half-knowledge is utterly dangerous. It becomes a stumbling block.

I would like to share a small experience. It was a few years ago when I was driving to my friend's house during the night. There were no lights over there. Suddenly a bump came, unnoticed. I was not very fast, but since the bump was not visible, I was not very slow either.

Consequently, my car collided with the bump badly. Thankfully, no harm was done, but my engine abruptly ceased functioning. I was unable to comprehend the events that transpired.

Subsequently, the car failed to start. I called my friend, and together we tried, but the engine didn't start. I parked the car besides the road. In the morning, my friend called his mechanic; he tried for an hour, but he also failed. He informed me that there seems to be a major problem with the engine. Presumably, the engine sustained some form of internal damage. Subsequently, I sought the expertise of another technician; nevertheless, his attempts were unsuccessful as well. He also concluded that the engine seems to be badly damaged internally. Lastly, I went to the authorized service station of the company. They sent their mechanic, and he started the car within one minute.

It was truly unexpected. I inquired as to what had transpired.

He replied, "The company has given an inertia switch at the bottom of the seat. In case of a major hit, this switch will disable the electric fuel pump and stop the engine. This is a precautionary measure provided in some cars, as after a collision or rollover, if the fuel pump continues, the fuel supply can create a fire hazard. In that scenario, the first thing is passenger safety, and hence the switch disables the electric fuel pump, thereby cutting off the fuel supply to avoid any fire. This is a safety feature. Since you hit the bump, the switch became active, which stopped the fuel supply, and your engine stopped. The moment I reset your switch, the car is again in normal mode and your engine started."

I indeed regretted wasting all my time with those naïve mechanics who concluded some major damage in the engine. If I had not consulted the authorized service station, they would have opened the engine of my car. What a terrible situation! Just imagine who was more expensive, the one from the authorized service station or the one from a local workshop.

In my life, I have encountered several situations when I was completely stuck because the persons, I sought advice from were not thorough in their work. Because of their incomplete knowledge, they reached conclusions that were erroneous, and finally, exacerbating the complexity of the case.

In order to become an expert, we need thorough knowledge I've witnessed folks chit-chatting in parks. They have advices for everyone, including the president of America. But unfortunately, they have no clue about their own lives. Totally disoriented in life. Hence, knowledge is the key to gain perfection in your work.

Now coming to the fifth quality, which is the most important quality to become an expert. The quality that is mostly lacking in a common man is "Concentration."

Let me go into detail about this important quality.

Concentration: Concentration means focusing all your energy only on one task or activity.

Among the five traits, this one has the utmost significance. Therefore, I have provided a comprehensive explanation of this quality.

Concentration is the key to mastery in this world. Concentration will not do anything less than miracles. All the experts in this world possess exceptional concentration.

I would like to share a remarkable example that I learned during one of my trips at Mumbai Airport.

Once, I was coming from Mumbai. Unfortunately, the flight was delayed. Next to me was an athletic-looking man. He looked quite experienced and energetic. Well, we started talking casually without introducing ourselves. Coincidentally, we started discussing on concentration.

He was related to cricket, and he said, "An individual with poor concentration will never be able to become a proficient batsman."

What he said startled me. As a common man, we think that to become a good batsman, you need to have good physical strength, strong arms, a good grasp of the game, and other such qualities. Sports have traditionally been associated with physical prowess. Why was concentration such a crucial component in becoming a proficient batsman? It caught me off guard.

In a trice, I asked him with my eyebrows raised, "Concentration!!! how do you feel that concentration is the most important quality for a good batsman?"

The answer that he gave was very interesting, which I would like to narrate in his own words.

He said, "In an international cricket match, the average speed of a fast bowler is around 145 km/hr. The distance between two stumps is 22 yards, i.e., 20.12 mtrs. Considering the speed of the ball at 145 km/hr, it takes less than half a second for the ball to reach the batsman. At this speed, the ball becomes nearly imperceptible. Numerous batsmen have admitted the challenge of perceiving the ball when faced with a fast bowler. By the time they try to see the ball, it has already passed away.

However, within this half a second, the batsman has to decide his course of action, whether he should play defensive or take a short. If he intends to take a shot, he must thoroughly evaluate the cricket field, taking into account the fielders' positions and the most advantageous location to execute the stroke. Within half a second, the batsman tries to understand the trajectory of the ball, decides how and in which direction to take the shot, and then mobilises his entire body to execute the right shot. The batsman must perform all these activities within half a second.

Furthermore, the batsman is not performing in isolation; rather, he is encompassed by thousands of admirers and critics within the stadium. Then there is an internal anxiety about scoring runs and the ultimate goal of winning the match. The pressure of making runs and the emotional sentiment to secure victory for their nation persist all the time in their conscious and subconscious minds. Consequently, the mind is replete with anxieties and distractions.

Considering all the above, the batsman has to perform only within half a second. The batsman has to first judge the ball, make the right decision, and then execute the correct action. If the batsman does not concentrate well, he will easily miss the ball, which may result in injury, or he may be clean-bowled. All this, which seems so easy, requires exceptional concentration."

He further stated, "I instruct my team that, first and foremost, they should develop their ability to focus. It is imperative that a batsman see the ball clearly, regardless of any potential distractions. If a batsman is unable to focus on the ball, all his efforts will be futile. Therefore, in order to strike a proper shot, one must be able to see the ball clearly and then decide how hard to smash the ball in order to cross the boundaries without getting into the hands of the fielders."

His words took me by surprise. Regrettably, I neglected to ask his name, but as we were departing, I enquired about his occupation, and very softly he said, "I am a coach to the Indian cricket team."

It was a short meeting with him, but it was quite enlightening.

However, not only in cricket but concentration is the fundamental element for achieving competence in any domain.

I recall some discourses from my father. When I was quite young, my father shared some of his thoughtful discussions. Basically, my father had asked a question to one of his friends, Mr. Sinha, whom I presumed had a high-ranking position at Reliance Industries, one of India's most esteemed organizations.

My father asked, "What specific criteria do you see when considering a promotion for someone in higher positions within your organisation?"

Mr. Sinha's response was extremely insightful, and my father would frequently share it with his peers.

Mr. Sinha responded, "In addition to qualities such as intelligence, experience, knowledge, and honesty, there are two particular qualities that I take note of.

1. Concentration.

2. Attitude.

He said, "Scientists discovered that the ability to stay focused can be an important indicator of a person's future success. Concentration means accumulating all your energy and working with one mind, body, and soul. People who have this ability to work with one mind, body, and soul have the potential to achieve extraordinary feats in any domain. They have the potential to become the extraordinary beings of this earth. A common trait among all successful individuals is their exceptional level of focus. Due to which they exhibit exceptional dedication to their work.

Individuals who lack the ability to focus well will deplete their energy reserves, rendering their other attributes such as intelligence, knowledge, and diligence entirely futile.

My father further asked Mr. Sinha, "But how do you check the concentration level of people? It's an internal thing. It cannot be measured by any instrument or gauged by the human mind easily."

Mr. Sinha continued with a very insightful response.

He said, "There are three things that consequently arise from good concentration.

1. **Accuracy and precision:** For people who work with concentration, their work will be precise, and it will be accurate by all means. They will meticulously focus on every minute details, which play a vital part in our analysis and decisions. They will ensure that nothing is left to assumptions. Their work will be very enlightening and accurate.

2. **Depth**: Individuals that engage in focused effort delve into the intricacies of the subject. Their work has profound depth and is immensely valuable.

3. **Thorough**: With concentration, a task executed will be complete and thorough in every respect. Generally, people work to the extent they can survive, but people who work with concentration work with all their heart and soul. Their work will be impeccable and devoid of any flaws. You can rely 100% on their work, and likewise, you can trust such people for any assignment given to them.

Finally, their work is not less than a master piece, which no other person can match to its standards.

The second most important quality is attitude. Your attitude is the most important factor in determining all aspects of your performance, especially in team building. People with a positive attitude are able to attract people towards them, successfully integrate them into a cohesive team, and eventually lead people and the organization towards growth and success. Such individuals, with their positive attitude, are capable of fostering values, culture, harmony, and a good team, benefiting both the firm and its employees. Hence, they become the right choice for higher-level jobs.

As a result, individuals who possess good concentration and attitude, which are critical for senior positions, will excel in five significant areas.

1. Decision taking ability.

2. Problem resolving skills.

3. Knowledge.

4. Team building.

5. Commitment to job responsibility.

Mr. Sinha's response was quite insightful and discerning.

Hence, if we intend to gain expertise, the most important quality is concentration.

Unfortunately, I've seen that most people struggle with concentration. They have trouble focusing and are prone to getting distracted very easily.

It's not that people are getting distracted, but rather they love to get distracted. In essence, people have a natural tendency to look for distractions.

Allow me to provide a succinct and practical illustration to clarify this topic.

Quite often, while going to my office in the morning, I have seen that when a small accident occurs on the road, people gather in large numbers. Most of the time, the accident is not severe, but the crowd is huge. There are hardly 5 to 6 people who come forward to help the victim, whereas all others are spectators. Even after everything gets normal, I have noticed that people still want to be around the scene. Even when everything is over, people do not intend to leave the scene easily. Probably now they want someone to talk about it. It is morning hours, and most of them are heading towards their office. It is imperative for them to reach their office, but they are still at the scene, wandering aimlessly. These people are not the ones who got distracted by the scene of the accident, but they are the ones who love to get distracted and are waiting for something to happen.

Likewise, it does not matter whether it is an accident on the road or a meaningless talk over an irrelevant topic; people take a lot of interest in it, as they love getting distracted. They prefer to engage in activities that are unnecessary and pleasing to them, consuming their precious time and energy, rather than doing what they are meant to do or what really matters to them. Hence, most people love to get distracted.

Why social media platforms are becoming more popular because people love to get distracted. These platforms provide individuals with a plethora of opportunities for distraction.

These distractions are nothing but a hole in your wallet. You are continuously losing your time and energy and, indirectly, money from these holes.

There are a few in millions who have realized the above facts, and they persistently pursue their goals with focus and refrain from getting distracted in their lives.

Allow me to outline few fundamental guidelines to enhance your concentration.

In order to concentrate effectively, follow the three basic rules:

1. Do what you love to do.
2. Eliminate distractions in life.
3. Perform one task at a time.

Do what you love to do:

When you do what you love to do, concentration comes effortlessly within such tasks. For example, if a person is practicing his dancing, which he loves to do, he will naturally focus all his attention. Concentration will occur effortlessly when we engage in an activity that we enjoy or are passionate about. While sitting with our beloved, we are totally absorbed within that moment. Time flies within a second, or we can say time vanishes during those delightful moments. Hence, when we do what we love to do, there is no limit to time; there is nothing more pleasing and fulfilling to us than performing those tasks. We get involved with our mind, body, and soul.

Concentration through strenuous efforts is one thing while to remain focused quite naturally is another. Hence, when we do what we love to do, concentration comes effortlessly, or, as we can say, concentration is a byproduct of love. Wherever there is love, all our energy and attention will flow inexorably in that direction. Hence, do what you love to do.

With concentration, not only we reach greater depths, but we also conspire the universe to act along with us and with all its cosmic powers. This is how people break world records. It is through concentration that people have achieved the impossible and done miracles in their lives. All discoveries, inventions, and innovations are a result of concentration. Through concentration, people have made the impossible possible; they have reached the unreachable.

Consequently, concentration is the paramount attribute that enhances the potency, efficacy, and efficiency of the mind. With a focused mind, you can learn and deliver more in less time, gain more with fewer resources, and maintain composure and stability even in chaotic situations. You may eventually achieve success far more quickly than you had anticipated.

Let's move on to the next topic, which is how to stay focused in life by avoiding distractions. Our ability to concentrate will naturally improve if we master this technique.

Eliminate distractions in Life: There are two types of distractions.

1. Internal Distractions.

2. External Distractions.

Internal Distractions: Our poor belief system, our laziness, our narrow mindset, guilts from our past deeds, apprehension about the future, emotional turbulence, and pursuit of gratification. etc. are all internal distractions.

External distractions: External distractions include social media, unpleasant external circumstances, lack of resources, criticism, inadequate support from family and friends, unfavourable market conditions, etc.

A list of a few distractions is provided below:

Internal Distractions	External Distractions
Laziness	Lack of resources
Worries	Poverty
Unfavourable Thoughts	Physical disturbance
Anger	Bad company
Stress	Vices
Addictions	Gadgets
Ego	Gossiping
Jealousy	Unfavourable Circumstances
Attachments	Lack of time
Bad Health	Illicit affairs
Negative mind set	Social media

Likewise, you can classify all the distractions into two categories.

One should not be concerned about external distractions if they have the ability to manage their internal distractions. This is mostly due to the fact that someone who possesses the willpower to manage internal distractions can manage external distractions with ease. Managing internal distractions poses a greater challenge.

External distractions may not be in our control all the time, but the influence of external distractions can be controlled. Hence, a person having control over internal distractions will not be affected by external distractions.

Further, after my discussion on this topic with hundreds of people, I discovered the biggest internal distraction is laziness. Even individuals who are good human beings and refrain from bad habits or vices become targets of their own laziness.

As you are aware, being lazy is a situation in which you are unwilling to make any effort.

A friend of mine posed the following question to me: "I don't drink, I don't overeat, I don't get angry over trifles, I don't speak lies, I never think negatively about anyone, I try to keep my heart clean, and having done all this, if I get up late in the morning, what is the problem? I am not causing harm to anyone."

I replied to him, "Getting up late in the morning is basically laziness. This laziness will impede your progress and consume your time and energy. Just imagine what will happen when you lose your time and energy. It may delay your success, and sometimes that delay may be indefinite.

Further laziness comes in different forms. Sometimes it provokes you to get up late, sometimes it prohibits you from doing your work thoroughly, sometimes it provokes you to waste your time on social media, sometimes it makes you inactive towards important matters in life, sometimes it provokes procrastination in you, sometimes it deprives you of the ability to identify the right opportunities, and eventually it makes you like a retired person. Therefore, protect yourself from your most formidable opponent, namely, laziness, which makes you sluggish and stagnant, resembling a lifeless body.

He listened to my response with some surprise, but he agreed wholeheartedly.

Hence, Dear Readers, the first thing you need to do in your life is avoid all forms of distractions that prevent you from concentrating.

Perform one task at a time: As Albert Einstein allegedly said, "Any man who can drive safely while kissing a pretty girl is simply not giving the kiss the attention it deserves."

Concentration means focusing all your energy on a single task. Nevertheless, if our energy is not fully concentrated on a certain task at that precise instance, our energy will still be wasted. For example, if a lady is cooking food while also managing household chores and assisting her children with their schoolwork all at the same time, what will be the outcome? Eventually, she will accomplish nothing. Neither she will make nice meals nor she will be able to aid her children fairly in their studies. She won't be able to perform the housework properly. It is certain that she will make errors, and ultimately everything will remain unfinished. She won't justify any of her tasks.

The question is why do individuals not focus on one activity at a time? The answer is very simple. This is mainly because we are unorganized. When we are unorganised, we fail to plan. When we fail to plan, we are confronted with a situation of crisis where multiple things come to us with the same importance. Everything becomes urgent, leading to conflicting priorities, beyond our control. Eventually, we are unable to properly focus on a single task.

Until we are organised, we won't be able to plan properly. Improper planning in our lives inevitably leads to creating a mess. Avoid such a mess, align your work properly, and effectively synchronise your efforts, with proper focus and concentration.

Mastery is the only key to abundance and to acquire mastery, it is important to have the ability to focus well, which entails dedicating oneself to a single task at a time.

Hence, friends, in conclusion, become an expert in your field. Without expertise, there is no other way to become rich in life. Work hard, work sincerely, work with concentration, gain thorough knowledge in your field, and once you gain expertise, believe me, wealth will flow abundantly into your life.

This world is ruled and enjoyed only by experts. Everything else is an endless struggle.

FROM WHERE DOES MONEY COME AND FROM WHERE DOES IT LEAVE

As I told you, money comes from skills or expertise, which means it comes from the intellect. But where does it go? It goes into expenses. However, it is not that simple.

If we pay attention to our expenses, you will find something very surprising. Most of the expenses are not on the things that we need in our lives, but on the things that we desire. The things we desire are the ones that we love from our hearts.

For example, we all need branded clothes, exotic holiday trips, luxurious cars, expensive gadgets, opulent houses, lavish feats, cocktail parties etc. However, after a short while, we become tired of these things and wish to replace them with new models. The initial euphoria of a new purchase soon fades, leaving behind a hunger for change and for something more, a never-ending cycle of desire and temporary satisfaction. Hence, this is a constant expense in our lives, both in a recuring mode and on a large scale.

Our major expenses in life are due to the things that our heart desires. Hence, if you analyse the entry and exit of money in an individual, you will discover the startling truth that money comes from the intellect and goes out from the heart.

The priority of our expenses is the one that our heart desires, not the one that we actually need in life. In order to earn money, we employ our full range of abilities and competence and harness our cognitive faculties and intelligence in a strategic manner, but while spending, we just do as our heart desires. It takes months or years to earn, but money seeps out within a blink of an eye. The channel through which money comes into our lives is quite narrow and difficult, while the channel through which money goes out is quite large and easy, totally unchecked, and uncontrolled.

It was a few years before I saw a motorcycle on the road while I was driving to my office. It was elegant and attractive. I felt tempted to buy it. Despite its high cost, I could easily afford it. Generally, I go by car to my office since it is quite far. I would never take the bike to my office, as the journey would be too uncomfortable considering the traffic and pollution. So, the only use of the motorbike would be when I run some errands in the evening.

I asked myself a genuine question: If I bought the bike, how much would I use it? The answer was quite simple, as follows:

- I would use it daily in the evening for some errands in the first month.

- In the second month, I would use it 3–4 times a week.

- In the third month, I would use it exclusively on weekends.

- In the fourth month, the motorbike would be lying in my backyard, occupying space, and requiring maintenance.

So, the question was: What would the motorcycle be worth? The answer was that, in the long run, the motorcycle would become a liability in my life.

Analyse your purchases with the wisdom of a detective, deeply and sensibly keeping your emotions aside, and decide what you actually need and what you don't. The dance with money is intricate and often fraught with psychological pitfalls. Often, we would find ourselves rationalizing a purchase we didn't need, driven by an emotional impulse rather than logical reasoning.

We need to have the ability to resist gratification. Till the time we do not have the uncanny ability to control our impulses, it is difficult to lay a strong foundation of wealth in life.

I have a friend of mine, whom I always advised to get a Mediclaim policy since he was married and had two kids. I even cited the benefits of the Mediclaim policy. However, he heard from one ear and then out from the other. After one year, someone was ill in his family, and he spent a huge amount. I would say half of his salary or say four times the premium of the Mediclaim policy. This happened twice. After these two experiences, he took the Mediclaim policy. However, in between, he bought an expensive mobile phone, some new expensive goggles, branded shoes, and so on, which was utterly unnecessary.

Money comes from the intellect and goes out from our heart. The heart, which does not know the right way to spend.

Below is the list of expenses that generally eat up our investments, especially in a middle-class person's life.

- Expensive car.
- Exotic travel and exclusive club memberships.
- Expensive mobile phones and laptops.
- Expensive clothes, watches, and other gadgets.
- Paying heavy interest on unnecessary loans.
- Health care costs in absence of required Insurances.
- Alcohol, smoking, and other addictions.

What compels a person to purchase an item they don't need? Imagine yourself strolling through a busy shopping mall. The scent of fresh leather from a boutique caresses your senses, and your attention is drawn to a dazzling watch in a showcase. What is it that makes your heart quicken and your palms itch to reach for your wallet? Is it the item itself, or is it the story you've subconsciously attached to it?

Often, our cravings are less about the objects and more about the experiences and feelings they symbolize. The leather jacket may whisper tales of adventure and freedom, and the watch may represent success and recognition. We don't just buy items; we buy the intangible dreams organizations promote in their commercial marketing.

Advertisements are not mere announcements of product availability; they are crafted narratives designed to burrow into your psyche. They touch on your deepest desires and vulnerabilities.

Instant gratification is a strong influence that triggers the release of dopamine in our brains, leading us to purchase unneeded items.

People are obsessed with the "now" and the "new." Eventually, all this leaves us with a heavier financial burden.

I know some of my middle-class friends, if you ask them to invest Rs. 10,000, they won't, but they have 40 to 50 shirts and trousers, 10 pairs of goggles, more than 10 pairs of shoes, and an expensive mobile phone, and they still keep adding more and more items unnecessarily. People will have money for their Saturday drink party, but if you ask them to have a Mediclaim policy, they won't have money. People have money to buy expensive mobile phone, but if you ask them to make some investment in life insurance, they won't. People have money to buy expensive cars, but if there is a lucrative opportunity to buy an asset, they won't take advantage of it. During weddings, people spend massively on show-offs, which is unnecessary. I have seen people taking loans for marriages or spending their lifetime savings. Most of the expenses are unnecessary.

The truth about strategic investment in a common man's life is that, it is almost nil.

As our income increases, our savings should also increase, but the fact is that instead of savings, our unnecessary expenses are increasing. People say there is inflation, but I bet our unnecessary expenses are much higher in comparison to inflation. The prices of things required for our daily needs have increased, but at the same time, the list of our desires has increased much more in comparison to inflation. This phenomenon is known as lifestyle inflation, where the increase in our income level simply leads to more extravagant spending. Unfortunately, lifestyle inflation is a subtle but influential phenomenon that traps even those with high incomes. Eventually, such types of expenses either don't leave any savings or sometimes put people in debt, and hence financial struggle continues throughout their entire lives.

Imagine a scenario where two individuals earn the same six-figure salary. The first succumbs to the siren song of luxury brands, the latest gadgets, and the allure of a lavish lifestyle. The second adopts a more frugal approach, investing prudently and living within their means. Over time, the contrast in their financial health becomes stark. The key to wealth, therefore, lies not in the size of the pay cheque, but in the habits and decisions that govern its use.

It's not the magnitude of your income that forges the path to wealth; it's the wisdom with which you steward it.

I remember that before 30 years, we used to have one landline phone in our house. Now everyone has a mobile phone. Most of them have two phones, which are expensive models. The landline phone was changed at least after five years. But people change their mobile phones within two years.

There used to be one television in every house. Now, in every room, there is one television.

To have one car in a family was a luxury, but now every member has his own personal car.

People used to have only one watch during their entire lifetime. However, now people have 4 to 5 watches, that too the expensive ones.

I can list hundreds of similar examples. However, I would like to ponder a question: "Has inflation gone up, or has our list of desires gone up? What has really made our lives so expensive—our needs or our desires?"

Check it; it is not the needs; it is the desires that have made life harder.

Practically, we do not have any control over our expenses, or, I would say, we do not have any control over our emotions. The moment our hearts desire it, we proceed. Even if our bank balance may not permit it, our credit card facilitates it. Finally, we end up paying heavy penalties or interest on credit cards.

If we keep the channel of money only through our intellect, we can balance our financial priorities. Hence, monitor your expenses, allocate a budget for everything, and spend wisely. The root cause of overspending is neither credit cards nor attractive things. It is our heart. Don't let your heart intervene with your financial decisions. Let your intellect decide what is the right way to spend.

Analyse your expenses. Don't spend on unnecessary things to make you look rich or just for gratification. Before you allow money to exchange hands, ask yourself: Do I need this? Why do I want this? How will this purchase align with my values and long-term goals? Adopt a mindset that prioritizes needs over wants, quality over quantity, and long-term benefits over short-term pleasures.

The simple way to spend wisely is to allocate a budget for everything and ensure your spending is within your means. This allocation involves more than just basic mathematics; it requires balancing desires with discipline. Within the confines of a budget, the concept of 'needs' versus 'wants' becomes starkly apparent. Creating a budget is the cornerstone of financial discipline. It's your personal blueprint that outlines where your money should go before it's even earned.

Review and adjust your budget on a regular basis, as life is an ever-changing landscape of needs and wants. Budgeting is about making conscious choices, distinguishing between needs and wants, and planning for both short-term expenses and long-term aspirations.

In the words of a wise sage, "Do not save what is left after spending, but spend what is left after saving." Embrace this philosophy, and watch as your financial portrait gains clarity and vibrancy with each passing day.

I am furnishing a list of general expenses that are inevitable in a common man's life.

- Housing expense: mortgage or rent.
- Electricity Bill.
- Car Expense: Instalment, general maintenance, and fuel cost.
- Groceries.
- Internet, cable connections, etc.
- Subscriptions to newspapers, magazines, and other OTT platforms.
- Insurance premium.
- Health care.
- Children's education or child care.
- Money for recreation.
- Emergency funds.
- Retirement funds.
- House renovation.
- Clothing.
- Unaccounted expenses.

Calculate the necessary expenses and determine the potential savings that can be converted into smart investments. A budget should not be a prison but a garden where your financial well-being grows. Allow yourself room to breathe and enjoy the good pleasures of this world that make life sweet and joyous. Yet, be cautious. Avoid getting indulged into lavishness that can strangle your savings.

Adopting a practice of mindful budgeting, helps us make clear and intentional decisions when faced with various desires. It's about recognizing the difference between genuine needs and fleeting wants, between lasting satisfaction and ephemeral pleasure. This journey is not about deprivation. It's about empowerment. It's about making choices that serve us, that bring us joy without the weight of regret.

Finally, don't let your money disappear through unnecessary expenses. Control it, control your heart, make smart investments, and multiply your wealth.

INVESTMENTS

As far as investment is concerned, the best time to invest money is during our youth. Studies and historical data show that individuals who start saving early and consistently often enjoy a more comfortable retirement. However, knowledge of the right investment comes very late, i.e., by the time we are old, we have lost that opportunity. Hence, it becomes inevitable to learn about investment as early as possible. Basically, knowledge about investment should be imparted in schools and colleges, but unfortunately, it is not. In the ever-evolving narrative of your financial journey understanding of investment is a paramount.

However, I'm going to provide all the details about investments and eventually show with equations whether they're profitable or not. Are these investments making money for you or for someone else? I will cover all the aspects, and then you decide: is it worth making the investment you plan to make, or should you consider an alternative option?

What is basically an investment? The answer is very simple. Investment is a way that you earn money on the money you have saved from your regular income.

Why investment is important:

Investment is crucial, as it has the potential to significantly increase your wealth. Secondly, it also protects your money from inflation. If your investments are good, they can multiply your wealth in the long run; conversely, if you fail to invest your hard-earned money properly, you risk losing it. Hence, it becomes prudent to learn about proper investment. However, first, we need to understand inflation. Without a proper understanding of inflation and how it affects our savings and investments, it will be futile to understand the value of investment. So, let's begin with the fundamentals:

What is Inflation:

Inflation is the increase in the prices of goods and services that we need in our daily lives. When prices inflate, things become expensive, and we need more money to buy them. This refers to the overall increase in prices and the corresponding decrease in the purchasing power of money. To illustrate, imagine you're at the grocery store. You fill your cart with the same items every week, but gradually, you notice that your bill creeps higher, even though the number of items remains unchanged. This is inflation nibbling away at the value of your money.

To keep the economy going, inflation is important to a certain level. To understand this, let's say if things are getting cheaper day by day, people will start reserving their money, as they know that the longer, they wait, the cheaper the products will become. Consequently, purchases will start to fall. When purchasing starts to fall, sales will fall, and businesses will decline, ultimately resulting into a recession. Thus, one-way inflation within a certain limit is good for market growth.

After a detailed analysis, the economists have suggested that an inflation rate of about 2 to 3% is important and essential for a good economy. Inflation will keep the market strong and stimulate growth.

On the other hand, inflation is a thief that takes a portion of your savings every day. It is a silent robber that erodes the value of your savings over time, turning today's dollar into tomorrow's dime.

Assume, for the moment, that you have deposited US$100,000 in a locker before ten years. The total inflation rate over the previous ten years in the United States has been almost 25%. This implies that in ten years, US$ 100,000 will become US$ 75,000. This indicates that there has been a yearly decrease of US$ 2,500. Therefore, each year, inflation takes $2,500 out of your portfolio. Thus, the day will come when our $100,000 USD will be almost worthless.

So, the first thing we need to check what is the inflation rate. Second, we must determine if our investments are outpacing the rate of inflation or not. If they are not, we are bound to lose our hard-earned money in the future.

Let's say a worker is earning US $ 2000 a month. His expenses are as follows:

1. House rent   : US $ 500
2. Food expenses   : US $ 500
3. Car loan, fuel and maintenance cost   : US $ 300.
4. Education fees of children   : US $ 200
5. Electricity and gas bill   : US $ 200.
6. Other miscellaneous expenses   : US $ 300
    Total   **: US $ 2000.**

Let's say the inflation rate is 5%, which means all the above expenses will increase to US$ 2100.00. If his salary does not increase to 5% but increases to only 3%, then there will be a deficit of 2%. i.e., US $ 40.00. In order to compensate for this extra expense, this person has to now borrow this money from someone or take a loan from the bank.

Hence, our income should increase more than the inflation rate, or else we will become poorer day by day. If our increments are not above the inflation rate, then it means our salary is going down. I have seen employees being happy with their increments and making parties, but if they compare their increments to the inflation rate, their salaries have actually remained the same. Companies are raising their product prices due to inflation because they are compelled to do so, and customers are bearing the cost. Unfortunately, employees do not receive a salary increase that exceeds the inflation rate. Even if their salary is increasing as per the inflation rate, it is actually not an increment; it is the same salary they were getting in their last year. This implies that there will be no increase in their savings. Hence, we should always see what the inflation rate is and accordingly evaluate whether our income is increasing proportionately or not. If not, it is time to change our job.

If your investments aren't providing returns equal to or greater than the inflation rate, you're probably in trouble. You'll find yourself making tough choices about what you can afford as inflation eats into your purchasing power. Therefore, investors should count on inflation and plan accordingly.

Causes for Inflation: There are mainly three reasons to cause inflation:

1. **Demand Pull Inflation:** This happens when the demand of a product is higher compared to the supply, which results in an increase in the cost of goods and services.

2. **Cost Push Inflation:** This happens when the cost of raw materials or some basic material like oil, transportation costs, electricity, etc. increases, which affects the production cost, and thereby the cost of finished goods increases, causing inflation. This can also happen as a result of supply disruptions caused by abnormal weather or natural disasters like cyclones, floods, pandemics, famine, or wars that damage large volumes of raw materials, thereby causing inflation in the finished goods.

3. **Built in Inflation:** This happens when demands for quality increase, resulting in new technology and machinery that increase the overhead costs. With changes in technology and higher skill sets, workers demand higher wages. Hence,

the cost of the products would increase with the increased overhead costs, thereby causing inflation.

How Inflation Impacts.

If your income stays the same while the prices go up, your purchasing power or your savings will reduce.

If your income goes up by the same rate as the inflation rate, then your purchasing power and savings will remain the same, but that will not make you richer in the future.

If your income rises by a percentage greater than the inflation rate, then your purchasing power and savings will both increase, and you will have more resources to become richer in the future.

Hence, from the above, it is important that our income should increase more than the inflation rate if we intend to become richer in the future. If this is not happening, then we need to seriously think about changing our profession, whether job or business.

Further, after retirement, people who have fixed incomes from fixed deposits will be impacted by inflation. Hence, we need to evaluate our income after retirement, considering the inflation rate.

Considering all the above, we need to beat inflation. We need to invest our money where it increases much beyond the inflation rate.

Where to invest:

At its core, an investment is the act of allocating resources, usually money, with the expectation of generating an income or profit. Investment vehicles vary in their characteristics, each carrying its own distinct risks and rewards.

But where do you begin? The investing sector is extensive and may seem overwhelming, offering several options such as stocks, bonds, mutual funds, real estate, fixed deposits, gold etc. Each carries its own set of risks and rewards within its own complexities.

To comprehend their nature, let's delve into the intricacies of four prominent investment types as follows.

1. Stocks, Bonds, Mutual funds.

2. Real Estate.

3. Fixed deposits in Bank.

4. Gold.

Let us begin with Stocks, Bonds and Mutuals funds and before we discuss let me clarify the complex terms like "market capitalization," "yield," "liquidity," and "volatility", often associated with the above investment in a simple and concise manner.

Market capitalization is the total value of a company's shares, reflecting its size. Yield refers to the revenue generated by an investment, such as the interest earned from a bond. Liquidity refers to the ease with which an investment can be converted into cash without impacting its market value, whereas Volatility quantifies the frequency and magnitude of an investment's price over a given span of time.

Stocks also known as equity, represent a partial ownership in a corporation. Units of stock are called "shares" which entitles the owner to a proportion of the corporation's assets and profits equal to how much stock they own.

Bonds are issued by governments or corporations in order to raise money. By buying a bond, you are giving the issuer a loan that they agree to pay you back along with the agreed interest over a period of time. Corporations, states, and governmental bodies utilize bonds to fund various projects and activities.

Mutual funds are collective investments that combine funds from various investors to purchase a diversified portfolio of stocks, bonds, or other securities, managed by professionals.

Imagine a bustling marketplace where each stall offers different fruits, vegetables, or grains, each with its own flavour and season.

Stocks are like apples and oranges—sometimes sweet with high returns in a booming market, but at times sour when the market dips.

Bonds, meanwhile, are more like grains, generally less thrilling but a reliable source of steady, predictable income.

Mutual funds resemble a vegetable salad, blending various vegetables to balance flavours and provide a diverse investment option for your portfolio.

Some investors advocate for stocks due to their potential for growth, citing stories of stock market success that have transformed modest investments into vast fortunes. Others advocate for bonds, emphasizing their relative safety and steady income, which are appealing in times of economic instability.

Mutual funds are commended for their diversity.

Historically, stocks have provided higher returns than most other investment vehicles. While bonds offer lower returns, but act as a buffer against market volatility, with long-term government bonds typically yielding 5-6% yearly approximately.

Mutual funds' performance varies widely depending on their investment strategy, but they offer an accessible way for individuals to gain diversified exposure to the markets.

How do you determine the course of action to take? Consider this: What are your financial objectives? Are you accumulating funds for a house, preparing for retirement, or establishing an emergency fund? Your goals will determine your investing approach, influence your willingness to take risks, and direct how you distribute your assets. It is important to carefully research and select investments that align with your financial goals and risk tolerance.

The most important point is to meticulously assess the risk associated with these investments, like an artist who can observe the minute nuances in the most complicated painting. The higher the profits, the greater the risk. Therefore, evaluate the risk factors thoroughly and ensure that you are capable of managing them even in the most adverse situations without experiencing anxiety and losing your sleep.

In order to mitigate risk, consider the power of diversification—the art of not putting all your eggs in one basket. By spreading your investments across different assets, you minimize the impact if one underperforms. Diversifying your investments across various assets not only adds depth to your portfolio but also acts as a protective measure.

Further investing isn't just about cold calculations and strategic manoeuvres; it's also about patience and perspective. The market will ebb and flow, rise and dip, and often take your emotions on a rollercoaster ride. This is a gamble fraught with peril. The key is to remain steadfast and focus on your long-term goals rather than getting caught up in short-term fluctuations. History has shown that a consistent, long-term approach often yields more fruitful results.

As you venture into the world of investing, arm yourself with knowledge. Read books, attend seminars, and consult financial advisors. Remember that in this digital age, a wealth of information is at your fingertips, but discernment is the key. Seek out reputable sources and never stop learning.

Remember, this is your hard-earned money. You can't leave it to hear and say. Either be an expert or take expert's advice in these matters. Thorough knowledge, deep research, proper vision, and risk calculation are the keys to making a good investment.

Finally, the most important thing is that the security of money is always more important than its profitability.

Real Estate:

Have you ever considered the ground beneath your feet as a source of wealth? Real estate is a longstanding and enduring domain of investment that exists beyond the physical structures of concrete and steel. It's a tangible asset—a piece that can be touched, seen, and felt. But what makes it such a compelling choice for building long-term financial stability?

Imagine a house. Not just any house, but a home that echoes with family laughter, shelters dreams, and stands as a silent guardian through the changing seasons. It's a cornerstone of your financial future. This is the essence of real estate investment—transforming brick and mortar into a foundation for wealth creation. Real estate is not just about properties but also about opportunities.

So, why does real estate remain an evergreen option for investors? Consider its resilience. While other assets can be volatile, swaying to the whims of the market, real estate possesses a unique steadfastness. It's not just about the space within the walls; it's about the land, a resource that's finite and inherently valuable. As Mark Twain wisely quipped, "Buy land; they're not making it anymore." His words resonate with a truth that's as relevant today as it was back then.

But how exactly does real estate contribute to financial stability? To understand this, we must look at the multifaceted ways real estate investments can generate income and appreciate over time. Rental properties, for instance, provide a steady stream of passive income—a monthly inflow that can grow with the right management and strategic planning.

Beyond the allure of passive income lies the potential for appreciation. Property values typically grow due to variables such as inflation, urban development, and demand. It's like planting a young tree in rich soil and seeing it develop into a strong oak tree. Over time, the initial investment might grow substantially, turning into a valuable asset that can be accessed by selling or refinancing.

It is crucial to approach real estate with a clear and informed perspective. Every investment involves risk, including real estate. Volatility in the market, difficulties in property management, and unforeseen repairs and maintenance might challenge your plans. It is essential to thoroughly investigate, comprehend the local market, and be prepared for unforeseen circumstances.

Real estate isn't just about the present; it's an investment in the future. It's a way to pass on wealth to the next generation, to provide a tangible asset that can support your loved ones long after you're gone. In a world where so much is fleeting, real estate offers a lasting legacy, a testament to your foresight and dedication.

In conclusion, real estate stands as a beacon for those seeking to create enduring wealth. It's a path paved with possibilities, but it demands patience, expertise, and thorough knowledge.

Fixed deposits:

Let us understand what the actual returns the bank gives us while we keep our money against fixed deposits and what is the impact of inflation on the returns.

Below is an example, considering the investment made in India. However, the equation that I have provided can be used to evaluate the returns anywhere in any other country.

First, we need to check the Cost Inflation Index. Below is the table that provides the Cost Inflation Index for India.

Sr. No.	Financial Year	Cost Inflation Index
1	2001-02	100
2	2002-03	105
3	2003-04	109
4	2004-05	113
5	2005-06	117
6	2006-07	122
7	2007-08	129
8	2008-09	137

Sr. No.	Financial Year	Cost Inflation Index
9	2009-10	148
10	2010-11	167
11	2011-12	184
12	2012-13	200
13	2013-14	220
14	2014-15	240
15	2015-16	254
16	2016-17	264
17	2017-18	272
18	2018-19	280
19	2019-20	289
20	2020-21	301
21	2021-22	317
22	2022-23	331

Let's say I have deposited Rs. 4300 in a fixed deposit at a rate of 6% compound interest. Let's check what are going to be the returns after 22 years.

Sr. No.	P. Amount	ROI	Interest Amt.	T. Amount
1	4300	6%	258	4558
2	4558.0	6%	273.5	4831.5
3	4831.5	6%	289.9	5121.4
4	5121.4	6%	307.3	5428.7
5	5428.7	6%	325.7	5754.4
6	5754.4	6%	345.3	6099.6
7	6099.6	6%	366.0	6465.6
8	6465.6	6%	387.9	6853.5
9	6853.5	6%	411.2	7264.8
10	7264.8	6%	435.9	7700.6

Sr. No.	P. Amount	ROI	Interest Amt.	T. Amount
11	7700.6	6%	462.0	8162.7
12	8162.7	6%	489.8	8652.4
13	8652.4	6%	519.1	9171.6
14	9171.6	6%	550.3	9721.9
15	9721.9	6%	583.3	10305.2
16	10305.2	6%	618.3	10923.5
17	10923.5	6%	655.4	11578.9
18	11578.9	6%	694.7	12273.7
19	12273.7	6%	736.4	13010.1
20	13010.1	6%	780.6	13790.7
21	13790.7	6%	827.4	14618.1
22	14618.1	6%	877.1	15495.2

P. Amount   **: Principal Amount**

ROI   **: Rate of Interest.**

Int. Amount   **: Interest Amount**

T. Amount   **: Total amount after one year.**

Hence after 22 years the total amount after compound interest would be Rs. 15,495.2.

You can calculate the total amount at maturity with the below formula also.

A   **: Amount at maturity.**

P   **: Principal Amount**

r   **: Rate of Interest**

n   **: Number of times Interest is levied in a year.**

CII   **: Cost of Inflation Index.**

Now evaluating the actual value of this money.

$$\text{Actual value of money} = \frac{\text{Total Amount at maturity}}{\text{Cost inflation Index}}$$

$$= \frac{15495.2}{3.31}$$

$$= 4681.3$$

Now calculating

$$\text{Net return} = \frac{(\text{Total amount-Principal amount}) \times 100}{\text{Principal amount}}$$

$$= \frac{(4681.3 - 4300) * 100}{4300}$$

$$= 8.86\%$$

Hence the net value of money kept in fixed deposit for 22 years against 6% compound interest, considering the cost inflation index will be 8.86% more than its original value.

Similarly, when you are keeping your money in a fixed deposit on a short-term or yearly basis, you need to check the interest rate. Suppose the rate is 5% per annum, it seems like a fair return. However, if the inflation rate is 6%, your FD returns become negative by 1%. You earn 5% from the deposit but lose 6% due to inflation. Thus, the actual value of your money declines.

Gold:

Further let us see what will be the returns if we have invested the same amount in Gold. The below table displays the approximate market value of 10 grams of gold in India from 2001 to 2022.

Year	Gold cost for 10 gms.
2001	Rs.4,300.00
2002	Rs.4,990.00

2003	Rs.5,600.00
2004	Rs.5,850.00
2005	Rs.7,000.00
2007	Rs.10,800.00
2008	Rs.12,500.00
2009	Rs.14,500.00
2010	Rs.18,500.00
2011	Rs.26,400.00
2012	Rs.31,050.00
2013	Rs.29,600.00
2014	Rs.28,006.50
2015	Rs.26,343.50
2016	Rs.28,623.50
2017	Rs.29,667.50
2018	Rs.31,438.00
2019	Rs.35,220.00
2020	Rs.48,651.00
2021	Rs.48,720.00
2022	Rs.52,670.00

After 22 years the value of Gold is Rs.52,670.00

Now evaluating the actual value of this money.

$$\text{Actual value of money} = \frac{\text{Value of gold after 22 years}}{\text{Cost Inflation Index}}$$

$$= 52670 \,/\, 3.31$$

$$= 15912.3$$

Now calculating net return

$$\text{Net return} = \frac{(\text{Total amount} - \text{Principal amount}) \times 100}{\text{Principal amount}}$$

$$= \frac{(15912.3 \text{-} 4300) \times 100}{4300}$$

$$= 270\%$$

Hence, as per the historical data, investing money in gold for 22 years would have given a return of 270%, whereas investing money in fixed deposits at 6% would have given you a return of only 8.86% after considering the cost inflation index.

Likewise, you can analyse the returns on your investments on short term and long-term basis.

Let us understand the benefits of investing in gold. This will provide us with a more accurate understanding of sound investments.

Benefits of Investment in Gold:

Gold is the oldest currencies in history, lasting for atleast 3000 years, whereas the British pound sterling is estimated to be about 1200 years old. On the long-term gold has never lost its value.

The basic five benefits of Gold as an investment are:

Less Risk and More value: Gold as an investment offers dual benefits. Lesser risk and more value in terms of wealth creation on long term. Gold's historical data has demonstrated these advantages. Whatever the circumstances may be—whether a market recession, political instability, or hyperinflation—gold does not lose its value and provides a perfect investment hedge.

Simplicity in Gold trading: Gold does not require any specialised knowledge or skills to buy or sell. Like diamonds, paintings, stocks, cryptocurrencies, and real estate, we need specialised knowledge. We need a lot of paper work, but for gold, no special paper work is required, except pay, take the invoice, and just buy it. Moreover, you can buy a small quantity as per your financial budget, and you can buy it from anywhere. Further, there is no locking period like fixed deposits; hence, you are free to buy and sell anytime. It's simple and easy.

Insurance against Inflation: Gold provides protection against inflation, and I would say it is your insurance against inflation. As mentioned earlier, inflation is inevitable, and if our money is stored only in the form of money, it is sure to reduce its value due to inflation, which means the money will depreciate in the long run. The best way to secure your money against inflation is by investing in a commodity that provides 100% protection from inflation. Gold is one of those commodities that provides total protection from inflation. Gold continues to hold its ground, retaining value and serving as a hedge against inflation and economic downturns.

Maintenance free: Gold does not deteriorate, corrode, or lose its strength like other metals. It does not require any maintenance, unlike real estate or property. Hence, gold, once you buy it, requires zero maintenance for storage. This is what makes gold so precious. Hence, for a common man, gold is the most suitable choice for investment.

Stability in prices: One of the most stable commodities. The stock market is quite vulnerable to market conditions, affected by people's sentiments or their point of views; hence, prices get affected very badly sometimes. Likewise, in real estate, properties in certain areas can reach a saturation point. However, gold value does not saturate and is impervious to people's sentiments. Even during pandemics, market recessions, wars, or other force majeure, gold prices are quite stable.

The above five qualities make gold the best choice for everyone and for anyone.

Considering all the above, below are the basic factors that determine a good investment:

1. Surpasses inflation and multiplies on its own accord.

2. Less maintenance.

3. Easy liquidity.

4. Secured and safe.

5. Globally valuable.

Investments are good for generating passive income. They multiply your wealth and provide you with remuneration when you do not have the capacity to work and earn. They secure your future. The way we work hard to earn well, similarly, we need to meticulously think about investing our hard-earned money. Otherwise, the money we save will be used by others, more for their own benefit rather than ours.

As we draw this chapter to a close, let us crystallize the key takeaways for a good investment. Conduct diligent research and diversify your portfolio to withstand market volatility. Maintain a steady temperament and rely on data and historical insights rather than emotional reactions. Simplify and understand the financial vernacular, and remember that investing is not a reactionary pursuit but a strategic one.

Your current investments are like seeds that have the potential to blossom into significant assets in the future with proper nurturing. The choice is yours, and the time to act is now.

However, engage with experts, immerse yourself completely and conduct a thorough research. The world of advanced investment strategies is not for the casual observer. It is a world where the astute investor, equipped with knowledge and daring, can find the means to elevate their financial portfolio to new heights.

I recall a strange story of an incompetent person named Rajiv Singh, who made millions in his life. His father had a restaurant. His father was highly successful. They were not very rich but they were like an upper-middle-class family. However, when Rajiv's father died, Rajiv took over his father's business, and he ruined everything. Basically, Rajiv was temperamental, rigid, and quite lean and mean. Eventually, the restaurant was closed. Due to Rajiv's incompetency, he could not start any other business.

His daily routine was to go to the club in the morning, do some exercise, gossip with his friends, and come back home. After that, he spent the entire day at home. In the evening, he again went to the club, played cards, gossiped with his friends, and returned home. At night, he used to take two pegs of whisky. This was his schedule for the majority of his life. I heard everyone saying that one day this man would become a complete broke in his life, which seemed to be quite true.

Surprisingly, after 15 years, the situation was just the opposite. He became richer than ever—significantly rich. People who made predictions about him were still struggling for money, and this man, who had practically done nothing in his life, became a stinking rich man. I became very curious to know about him.

Serendipitously, one day I met one of my classmates, Kalpesh, who turned out to be Rajiv's part time accountant. As we were conversing about money, I asked Kalpesh how Rajiv, despite all the incompetencies, multiplied his wealth so significantly.

"Sukhvinder, apparently what you or people feel about Rajiv is not true. The truth is far beyond your comprehension." stated Kalpesh with a smile.

My curiosity piqued and I asked, "Kalpesh, I am curious to know how this man managed to amass such a substantial amount of wealth."

In response, Kalpesh said, "Sukhvinder, Rajiv is a genius as far as money matters are concerned. He has some worthy qualities."

"What qualities?" I asked.

Kalpesh replied, "Sukhvinder, Rajiv works only one or two hours a day, and throughout the year he will make two or three deals. But he manages to make millions within a couple of years from those deals. He works with vision.

A few years before, an NRI (Non-Resident Indian) came here to sell his property. I was involved in that matter as one of my clients,

Mr. Dev, was interested in buying that property. Several discussions were carried out between the NRI and Dev, but finally the discussions failed to materialise. The NRI was too greedy. The fair price of the property was INR 5 million, but he expected INR 5.5 million.

Somehow, Rajiv came to know about this unsuccessful deal.

He called me at night. When I reached, he was having his scotch. He asked me to draft a small agreement pertaining to this deal, leaving the price column blank. He had already arranged the meeting with the NRI at 9:00 a.m., the next day. He asked me to accompany him. In the morning, we went to meet him. Within ten minutes, Rajiv finalised the deal for INR 5.3 million. The agreement was signed, and Rajiv gave him the advance.

I told Rajiv that he had paid more than the current value of the property.

"Kalpesh, one day the value of this property would be ten times what I am paying right now." Rajiv remarked at that time.

Surprisingly, within ten years, the property prices skyrocketed and the price of that property went to INR 100 million.

Sukhvinder this individual, possesses a distinct understanding of financial matters; consequently, he capitalises on prospective opportunities with his astute abilities.

During the pandemic, we all invested in the stock market, as it was a good opportunity. Rajiv also invested. I sold my stocks with returns of 30% to 40%, and I was extremely happy. However, Rajiv did not sell his stock, and he patiently waited. Eventually, most of his stocks multiplied atleast 4 to 5 times. Once again, with his vision and patience, his investments skyrocketed.

He is a very patient man in money matters. He knows when to invest and when to sell.

I still remember a few years ago, when his family insisted on buying a new car, I was there at that moment. His family was quite agitated with him, as he refused to buy the car. I also persuaded Rajiv, to buy a new car. It was not a big deal for him.

However, he said, "Kalpesh, if I buy a new car, I would lose the opportunity to buy a small shop with that money I have already planned, and I don't want to lose this prospective opportunity. Moreover, I don't need a new car. I stay at home all the time. We are only three people: me, my wife, and my son. It is once a month that we go somewhere out. So, what is the point of spending the money on a new car? I already have one. It is enough for my needs."

Finally, he bought that shop, and he continued with his 10-year-old car. Within a few years, as the price of that shop appreciated, he can buy at least five new-brand cars now. Sukhvinder it is not enough to simply invest; one must do so wisely, with a discerning eye for opportunity and a steadfast heart against the siren calls of short-term gratifications.

Sukhvinder, what you and I consider to be working hard, is basically struggling for pennies, which is a never-ending task. However, Rajiv does not do that; he does not work for pennies; he works smart to make millions.

People think Rajiv does not work at all, but Rajiv always says, "Those people who work more, either they work for others or they compel themselves to work more by comparing themselves with others. But I work exclusively for myself, without comparing myself to others, so I work less and earn more."

This is his philosophy. Neither he compares himself with others nor is he concerned about what people say about him. Rajiv does not bind himself with the anxiety of not having enough or the relentless comparison to others who seem to possess more. He does not worry about keeping up with the Joneses."

I interrupted Kalpesh and asked him, "What does 'Keeping up with the Joneses' mean?"

Kalpesh smiled and said, "Sukhvinder people who try to keep up with the Joneses are people who believe it's important to show that they're as successful as others, such as their wealthy neighbours. These individuals always want to own the same costly items as their friends or neighbours have, even though they can't afford them easily."

It was a good idiom that I learned. Many individuals suffer from this mental behaviour.

Kalpesh continued, "Sukhvinder what Rajiv makes in a year, with his ability in identifying the right opportunity and creating valuable assets, we cannot make that money during our entire life. Being honest, being hard-working, and disciplined is a good thing, but having the skills to multiply your wealth is a different art. Till the time you don't learn that art, you will never become rich.

People evaluated Rajiv with his old car and with his unsuccessful past, and hence they totally underestimated him.

But Rajiv knows how to save money, where to invest it, and finally, how to multiply it. He is a maverick and has an uncanny ability to manage and multiply his wealth in ways that seems almost serendipitous.

Some people think they are working hard, but they may be working blindly for the benefit of others. You need to work smart and work for yourself. As far as investments are concerned, one needs to be smart. Rajiv is not a hard-working guy like you and me, but the fact is, in the realm of sound investment decisions, you need to be sensible and strategic like Rajiv, rather than being hard-working."

Well, it was really interesting to know about Rajiv. This story is about maximizing your wealth, not through hard work, but through opportunities and valuable assets. I agree with Kalpesh; you need to become smart as far as investments are concerned. This means identifying the right opportunity, taking calculated risks, making the right investments, and having the patience to let our investments grow to their maximum. For this, you don't need to work hard; you need to be more sensible in such matters. It demonstrates that with the right blend of vision, thorough knowledge, and strategic decision-making, your small actions can serve as a formidable engine of wealth creation.

As we approach the conclusion, it is important to synthesize the key takeaways.

1. Vision.

2. Patience.

3. Spare money for good investments.

4. Ability to create profitable assets.

5. Opportunistic.

The journey to wealth through assets is one of vision, patience, learning, and the courage to build not just structures but also legacies.

The pursuit of wealth is not a sprint; it is a marathon, requiring patience, endurance, and the foresight to look beyond the immediate horizon. Just as the sculptor sees the statue within the marble, the astute investor perceives the market's potential within the market. This chapter is dedicated to the cultivation of an investor's mindset, one geared towards long-term success, and the principles that underpin such a strategic approach.

In conclusion, investing is a long-term endeavor rather than a short-term one. It's a journey of knowledge, awareness, and patience. If saving is about preserving your money, investing is about growing it. Begin on a modest scale, if necessary, but start. By investing each dollar, you are creating a more stable financial future where your money is actively working for you.

Therefore, earn ethically, invest prudently, and enjoy the rewards lavishly.

ASSETS

What are assets: They are the foundation and stalwarts of your wealth pyramid. They stand as bastions against financial uncertainties and provide a robust base for the framework of lasting wealth. In simple terms, assets are valuable items, whether tangible or intangible, that provide future financial benefits by all means. Without assets, no one has ever become rich in this world. Hence, assets are the bedrock for strengthening not only your economic resilience but also promising a bountiful return to your personal wealth.

Assets are basically those valuable things, having the following basic characteristics:

- Assets add value to your overall wealth.

- Inflation does not affect assets.

- The value of assets appreciates with respect to time.

Assets basically add value to your wealth. For example, in accounting, a car can be considered as an asset, but it actually does not add any value to your wealth. The moment the car comes out of the showroom, its value decreases, and it further depreciates from time to time. Hence, a car cannot be considered as an asset. It can be a necessity in life, but not an asset that contributes financial value to your overall wealth.

Similarly, a house, for instance, does not only provide you shelter or a roof over your head; it may also appreciate over time, becoming a potential source of wealth for the future. Hence, a house or any such property is a real asset that provides you with financial benefit and overall stability in your financial landscape.

Assets can be classified basically into two categories:

1. Tangible assets.

2. Intangible assets

Tangible assets are physical substances that can be seen, touched, and felt. In accounting, an asset is defined as a current economic resource that has the potential to produce future economic benefits. Tangible assets are like your property, gold, art, etc. These things do not depreciate with time, do not get affected by inflation, and, at any given point, provide financial benefits.

Conversely, an intangible asset has no physical nature. It cannot be touched or felt, but they are no less valuable than tangible assets. Intangible assets are like stocks, bonds, mutual funds, intellectual property, goodwill, etc. Intangible assets may be more elusive to the eye, yet they often harbour the power for significant financial growth.

The most important asset in your life is your own health. It's a vital asset that allows individuals to think consciously, work productively, and enjoy the fruits of their labor adequately. Healthy individuals are more likely to secure employment, become eligible for promotions, and receive greater compensation. Likewise, in business, individuals in good health may propel their firm to great success. On the flip side, poor health can become a significant barrier to achieving and maintaining financial success, as it may limit one's ability to work or lead to substantial medical expenses that deplete savings.

Hence, health is the most crucial asset for financial stability in life.

In conclusion, assets by all means and in every form are the lifeblood of personal wealth. They are the resources that, when wisely acquired and managed, can yield prosperity and security. The value of your wealth does not lie in the figures, but in the stability of your wealth. Therefore, assets are the seeds from which your economic stability will grow.

LIABILITIES

❧

On the other hand, liabilities are just the flip side of assets. Assets put money in your wallet, and liabilities take money out of your wallet. Liabilities are the ones that decrease your wealth by various means. Liabilities are simply debts or obligations that arise during the course of financial transactions. They encompass loans, mortgages, credit card debts, and any other form of money that we are legally obligated to repay.

However, liabilities are inevitable. There is not a single individual in this world who lives without a liability. Just like Benjamin Franklin says, **"Nothing is certain except death and taxes."** So are liabilities, certain and unavoidable in our lives.

There are four basic needs of the human body, what we call as the physiological needs, like food, shelter, clothes, and medical aid. Similarly, there are several basic needs of a human mind—what we call as our psychological needs—like love, security, society, stimulation, recognition, spiritualism, purpose, morality, etc.

To fulfil the above basic needs, every human being will pursue them to any extent and eventually invite liabilities in life.

Everyone needs a good house—a family home brimming with laughter and love. Homeownership is the quintessential dream of every individual in this world. Similarly, with awareness of health and eating habits, people need proper food. Likewise, clothes represent one's personality and exhibit their aura and status. Hence these essential needs cannot be ignored.

Further, medical aid is inevitable in today's world. Without proper medical aid, human existence would be difficult and sometimes painful. The population is increasing not because the birth rate has gone up but due to the fact that death rate has gone down. From the moment a baby is conceived in a mother's womb, a human being needs medical assistance. Hence, these basic needs are essential and have become a major expense.

Further, as Aristotle said, "Man is a social animal. He cannot survive in isolation." As a result, not only a home is important, but society or the surroundings are also important. Apart from surroundings, socializing with the right kind of people, especially the loved ones, is an important part of life. Apart from socializing, humans consistently strive to fulfil their other psychological requirements. Hence, to fulfil all these affairs, we need money. Often, to fulfil these needs, we unintentionally invite liabilities into our lives without diligence and care.

Hence, it is imperative to learn how to handle this important financial aspect so that our liabilities do not impact our financial well-being negatively. Liabilities can obstruct us with their negative potency, or they can be the cords that bind together a future of stability and success. It is our duty to understand liabilities from diverse perspectives, to respect their power, and to wield them with care.

The most common liabilities in today's world are as follows:

1. Home loan.

2. Car Loan.

3. Credit card expenses.

First, a house is something that transforms into a home with loved ones. A home is not just the value of the property—land and structure—it is much beyond that. It has an emotional value that is much beyond the materialistic value.

In a country like India, where people lived in joint families in the past, but now with the concept of a nuclear family, every couple wants a different house. Hence, there has been a drastic increase in demand for new houses. With population growth, demand for new houses has further increased significantly. The real estate business in India will be booming in the next few years. Hence, home loans will increase in near future.

Now the question is whether home loans are safe and secured for financial growth or not.

I have discussed this topic with a lot of financial consultants. The best answer that I got, I would like to share with my readers as follows:

Buying first home is essential, and looking at the property as it appreciates over time seems like a prospective deal. However, the mortgage, which is a massive debt, requires monthly payments for an extremely long time. What if the market dips and the income declines? Could this dream turn into a nightmarish pit where the income discontinues and the burden of repayment becomes difficult?

The answer is that if there is only one source of income in the house and the mortgage is fulfilled by only one source, then it becomes a risky affair.

Hence, to mitigate this problem, it is imperative that the wife and husband both have their own sources of income. Each income should be sufficient to cover the mortgage and other living expenses in the event that one income discontinues. Due to the long duration of these loans and market uncertainties, there is a possibility that one income source may not remain steady for the entire loan duration. Hence, in that situation, the other income will act as a buffer and take care of the liability.

Further, insure the total loan amount to protect against unforeseen circumstances. In case of unpleasant demise, where one source of income stops permanently, the burden should not come solely to the other person.

Moreover, knowledge is the rudder that keeps the ship on course. Understanding terms and conditions, interest rates, mortgage structure, and associated penalties can empower individuals to make well-informed decisions.

Hence, a significant loan should be supported by two income streams, adequate insurance coverage, and a comprehensive analysis of the property before investing to ensure seamless loan repayments and satisfactory returns.

However, as far as credit cards are concerned, credit cards should be used as a mode of payment, within the limits of your budget. For example, I use my credit card for online shopping. My purchases are strictly limited to my budget and are within the balance available in my bank account. I have never used my credit card as a loan facilitator. When credit cards are used beyond one's budget, people fail to make timely payments, attract penalties, interest accrues, and the person finds himself in a tightening vise of financial pressure.

Hence, any expense or loan should be taken with diligence and care. Liabilities should be a stepping stone towards your financial growth and not become a shackle that constrains your cash flow, leaving you teetering on the edge of insolvency.

In conclusion, liabilities are not inherently good or bad. They are tools that, when wielded with care, can build empires and secure futures. Yet, when handled recklessly, they can just as easily ruin fortunes. The savvy individuals will respect the power of liabilities, harnessing them to fortify rather than undermine their financial well-being.

Remember, financial freedom is not just about the assets you accumulate but also about the liabilities you avoid or manage well. The choices you make today will echo through your financial future. As we close this chapter, let us ponder a simple yet profound question: Are your liabilities working for you, or are you working for your liabilities? The answer to this question could redefine your financial journey.

In conclusion, managing liabilities is an ongoing endeavour, a symphony that demands both attentions to detail and an analysis on a broader financial landscape. Choose your strategies wisely with vigilance and foresight.

WHY RICH BECOMES RICHER AND THE POOR BECOMES POORER

Why do the rich become richer and the poor become poorer? In order to understand this, we first need to understand the fundamentals of money. First, let us understand what makes someone rich in life. What is it, precisely, that makes someone wealthy? There are two basic elements that make someone rich in life. They are as below:

1. Expertise.

2. Assets.

As I already explained, if you want to earn more money, then skills will not work; you need to have expertise in your field. However, expertise will give you active income, not passive income necessarily. Active income means that till the time you are active, you earn. The moment you cease to work, your income stops. Hence, if you intend to remain wealthy in life, you need to generate passive income. Passive income means money keeps coming, even if you stop working. Passive income primarily originates from assets such as the following:

1. Rental income from property.

2. Investment in gold.

3. Investment in stocks.

4. Income from digital products like online courses, online videos, etc.

5. Royalty income from books, singing, patents, trademarks, copyrights, etc.

Now coming to the main question: why do the rich become richer and the poor become poorer? The answer is very simple.

As you are aware, inflation is inevitable. What does inflation do? It simply increases the price of the goods and services. Therefore, it also increases the value of the assets. What does a rich person have, mainly in comparison to poor people? A rich person has a greater number of assets in life. Therefore, the values of assets like property, gold, stocks, etc. would rise due to inflation. Consequently, a wealthy person gets richer. At the same time, a poor person who does not have any assets only has liabilities. Liability refers to costs, financial obligations, or expenditures. As costs increase day by day due to inflation, the poor will become poorer

The equation is very simple: people who have assets will automatically become richer day by day, and people who have no assets will become poorer day by day. This is simply due to inflation.

So, inflation is a blessing to the rich and a curse to the poor. This also means that if you want to take advantage of inflation, you should try to generate more assets in your life. The more assets you have, the wealthier your life will be.

As per the above, only those who are building more assets in their life will become wealthy. In contrast, people who create more liabilities will become poorer day by day.

More the assets   More you are moving towards richness.

More the liabilities   More you are moving towards poverty.

I would like to share a small example. Tom and Harry both have US$400,000 with them. Tom buys a new sports car, an expensive mobile, and goes on a lavish trip to the world's most expensive place. At the same time, Harry has invested that money in property. He is getting a steady stream of rental income, plus his property is appreciating every year.

After 5 years, the value of Tom's car is hardly 10%, plus he has lost all his wealth to unworthy expenses. As far as Harry is concerned, the total wealth generated due to rental income and appreciation of his property is almost double the initial amount. Hence, Harry has become financially stronger, whereas Tom has lost his precious wealth over worthless expenses.

The above example applies to all of us. Are we creating more liabilities, more expenses, or more assets? What are we really doing with our income?

The fundamental equation about wealth is that those who generate more assets will ultimately become wealthy, whereas those who engage in excessive spending will continue to face financial hardship throughout their lives.

People who start investing and creating assets in early life will become rich at the time when they need money the most. Hence, they will live rich. People who do not invest their money properly will keep struggling throughout their life and may end up into poverty.

Further, I would like to highlight some important piece of note for the common man. This world is like a paradise, but as far as the financial world is concerned, people can be quite selfish. In this world, people don't give money to those who need it very badly; on the contrary, they may take advantage of them. I have seen individuals being exploited in the workplace. Hence, start making assets so that when you need money badly in life, you don't get exploited, stressed, or fall into debt.

It is important that parents should provide proper financial education to their children to help them establish clear financial objectives once they begin working. Increase your assets and reduce your expenses and liabilities. Take the advantage of the natural factors to multiply your wealth easily. Become rich and richer effortlessly by understanding the sound principles of this chapter.

FEW RECOMMENDATIONS TO HEALTHY FINANCIAL GROWTH

1. Take the necessary insurances to avoid heartbreaking bills. Insurance can prevent a liability from metastasizing into an uncontrollable force that wreaks havoc on your financial well-being.

2. Do not spend unnecessary money on expensive gadgets. Save money.

3. Save time. Time is money.

4. Don't compare yourself with others. It is the biggest distraction.

5. Save your energy. It is difficult to act and succeed without energy.

6. Maintain your health. Eat, sleep, and exercise consciously. Health is your biggest asset in life.

7. Always remain in a happy mood. Your productivity, efficiency, and quality will increase drastically.

8. Be in good company. Avoid negative people. Negative people are a big distraction and a liability in life, no matter if they are your friends, relatives, or neighbours.

9. Cultivate the habit of reading books. Become a person of wisdom rather than only having educational degrees.

10. Avoid wasting time on social media. Instead, explore opportunities to make smart investments.

INSURANCE

৩৩

I generally ask people, when you see a person riding a motorbike, who is more important, the bike or the person? Unanimously, everyone gives me the same answer, i.e., "The rider."

But unfortunately, the bike has insurance, but the rider does not. People know, but unfortunately, they don't realize. Moreover, the most surprising thing is that they will spend money on expensive accessories on the bike or on their cars, but they will not take any accidental insurance for themselves. People buy what they desire, but they don't buy what they actually need in life.

In the journey of financial growth, the most important point is shielding your wealth from the uncertainties of life and the unexpected twists of fate. While watching the "Discovery" channel, there was a common saying: **"Disasters happen when they are expected the least."**

Like **"Change is the only constant of life,"** similarly, **"Uncertainties are the cardinal truth of life."** The one who has accepted is wise and mature, and the one who has not realised this universal truth will be a loser one day.

Hence, we all need a shield to protect our assets from the sieges of life's uncertainties. What is that shield? We all know, "Insurance."

What exactly is insurance? Insurance is basically a contractual agreement, known as a policy, in which an insurer agrees to compensate the policy holder for any losses resulting from particular unforeseen events, in the event of a disaster.

The best thing the world has provided is "Insurance." The worst thing is that people have failed to understand its importance, and Insurance is the last priority in their lives.

Once, I was talking to one of my friends who was sharing with me about his wife, how they met, how they fell in love, and how they finally got married. Now he has a child, and he is extremely happy with his family. He told me that he loves his wife and child the most and that he cares a lot for them.

Suddenly, I asked him, "Do you have a life insurance?"

Surprisingly, he asked me, "Why?"

I responded, "God forbids, if you become incapacitated or you depart untimely from this world, who will look after your family after your death?"

He remained silent for some time and replied, "Sukhvinder, this is a hypothetical situation. There is hardly any possibility of such an event."

I said, "Okay, let me correct you slightly. The chances of untimely death may be less, but since death is certain, the possibility of death persists 100%. Do you agree with me?"

He replied, "Yes."

I continued, "It is only the time that we do not know. Since we do not know the timing, death seems like a suspense. Hence, this issue still does not become less important when the lives of our loved ones are at stake due to this suspense or let's say due to our ignorance."

He replied slowly, "Yes, maybe you are right."

I then asked, "You mentioned that you care about your wife and son. As I told you, if something happens to you, what will your wife do? Without the insurance, she would be facing not just grief but potential bankruptcy. How will she manage to get money to look after your child? How will she survive?"

He became pensive and said, "I don't know."

I said, "If you really care about her, then you need to take an insurance on priority. Love them sensibly and not blindly."

He said, "OK," in a hushed voice.

Within a few days, he came to me and said, smilingly, "I have taken the insurance."

Life is as unpredictable as a tempestuous sea. What would happen to your family if your income suddenly stopped? Life insurance is the answer to this daunting question, providing peace of mind, financial stability, and safety to your loved ones.

There are different types of Life Insurances. Just like to name a few:

Term life insurance: Term life insurance offers protection for a specific timeframe—usually 10, 20, or 30 years.

Whole life insurance: As steadfast as the mountains, whole life insurance endures for your entire lifetime.

Universal life insurance: Universal life (UL) insurance is a form of permanent life insurance with an investment savings element plus premiums and a death benefit that are flexible.

Health Insurance: In the battlefield of health, your greatest ally is health insurance. With healthcare costs soaring to dizzying heights, a single illness or injury can plunder your savings. Health insurance steps in to cover medical expenses, from routine doctor's visits to emergency surgeries.

Auto Insurance: Auto insurance is the armor around your vehicle, protecting you against the financial repercussions of traffic accidents. A comprehensive policy provides coverage against third party liabilities and loss or damages caused to the insured car due to accidents, vandalism, fire, theft, manmade and natural calamities.

Accidental Insurance: Accidental insurance is a form of insurance policy that offers a payout when people experience injury or death due to an accident. Some accidental insurances also compensate the loss of your income while you are unable to work.

If we don't plan for the uncertainties of life, the consequences are dire. Without preparation, individuals may find themselves in a financial freefall, struggling to pay bills, and forced to liquidate assets at a loss. Financial dreams of prosperity could be pushed back indefinitely, and the financial stability that once seemed guaranteed could evaporate like a mirage.

In conclusion, insurance is not a luxury; it is a necessity, ensuring that a crisis does not escalate into a financial catastrophe. Insurance is not merely a financial tool; it is a symphony of protection that plays in harmony with your life's goals and dreams. Insurance is the invisible shield that protects your financial base from potential calamities. It is an act of foresight and responsibility. It safeguards your assets, secures your future, and provides peace of mind for both you and your loved ones.

Evaluate your need for various types of insurance, including health, life, and property. It's crucial to have adequate coverage that aligns with your life stage and personal circumstances.

Ensure that, come what may, your wealth, your family, and your peace of mind will stand resilient against the tides of uncertainty.

Safety of your family is your first priority, and safeguarding your wealth for their survival is equally important.

GOALS

Albert Einstein was on a train one day when the railroad ticket-checker began walking down the car, checking tickets. However, as the ticket-checker approached, he watched Einstein search his wallet, unable to find his ticket. Frustrated, Einstein then checked each of his pockets, but still no ticket was found.

Einstein was more and more agitated with himself as he went through his briefcase, still unable to find his ticket. The ticket-checker finally made his way to Einstein's seat.

"Albert Einstein," he said, laughing. "Everyone knows who you are, and I have full confidence in your integrity and honesty, and I am sure you will never travel without a ticket. There's no need to show me your ticket."

"No, sir, that's not the problem," said Einstein. "The problem is that I can't remember where I'm going."

The story is probably apocryphal, as it's also been attributed to other such dignitaries.

However, the fact is that without goals, our lives would be the same: travelling in a train but not knowing where we are going, despite being intelligent and capable. We would not be living our lives, but wasting them. Once we have goals, we can say we are not only living but also leading our lives.

How to set your Goals.

To understand success, we should indeed know what the starting point of success is and what the finishing point is. Without this basic knowledge, it would be difficult to understand where to start our journey and how long to continue it. Let me make this very clear.

Success is a journey that starts with your dreams and continues to the point where you deserve them. Having dreams is the starting point, and elevating yourself to the level you deserve is the final stage. The foremost important thing is "Dreams." Without dreams, there is no journey. However, all dreams are not goals. So, what are goals? Are all our wishes or dreams "**Goals**?" The answer is:

"Only those dreams that elevate you in your life while pursuing them and after their achievement are Goals, everything else is meaningless."

When you set your goals, make sure that they are very high. When I was young, I had the goal of having my own Mercedes or BMW car. But later, it seemed like toys to me. Hence, your goals should be so high that such things should be the by-products of your goals.

"The quality of your Gaols will determine the Quality of your life."

Your Goals should be RICH

1. R-Realistic

2. I-Inspirational

3. C-Committable.

4. H- Honourable.

Some people say that your goals should be smart. Smart means S-Specific, M-Measurable, A–Achievable, R–Relevant, and T-Time bound. I appreciate this definition. Both the definitions are meaningful and good, though I personally feel the most important thing in your goal is H: – Honourable.

Any goals you set, should be honourable for your parents, for your children, for complete humanity, and for the next generation.

**"Try not to become a man of success,
but rather try to become a man of value."**

– Albert Einstein

Secondly, most of the time, goals are vague. For example, "I want to be rich" lacks the backbone of specificity. Instead, envision your goal with precision: "I aim to save $30,000 for a down payment on a home within two years." Do you see the difference? One is but a wisp of a dream; the other is a blueprint for action.

Three basic things that are important to set your goals are as follows:

1. Moral.

2. Wisdom.

3. Focus.

The first important thing is morals. Whatever goals you set, first of all, check whether they are morally right or not. Anything that is morally incorrect, all work done will be disastrous; energy consumed will be enormous and finally lead to regrets in life.

Well, whatever dreams you have, write them down and check whether they add any value to your life or make it miserable. Thieves also have goals to make a bigger robbery. However, this is a crime and an immoral act, and one day it will certainly ruin their life. Hence, analyse your goals on moral grounds and never do anything that is unethical.

Then comes wisdom and focus. Wisdom will give you the right direction to pursue your goals. Focus will give you enormous energy and depth.

Thus, the journey starts with you and ends with you. We have to start it with our dreams and pursue it until we truly deserve it.

The path to financial prosperity is paved with clearly defined goals, with each step taking a purposeful stride. Setting financial goals is an art, a delicate balance between ambition and realism. Let your values guide your goals, for they are the stars by which you navigate the sea of financial decision-making.

As you define your gaols, ask yourself: What skills can I develop that will open doors for me? How can I demonstrate my worth in a way that commands a higher price? Am I willing to invest in my education to elevate my potential? The answers to these questions are the first steps on your path to financial empowerment.

Embarking on the journey towards financial prosperity begins with setting the right goals. These goals are not just figures on a bank statement; they are the embodiment of our values, aspirations, and the life we dream of leading.

Your primary objective is to set achievable, motivating financial goals that resonate with your personal values and dreams.

To effectively set your goals, you'll need several key steps:

- Self-reflection and understanding your values.
- Assessing your current financial situation.
- Dreaming big and setting long-term goals.
- Breaking down these long-term goals into small achievable goals.
- Developing skills and a plan of action.
- Regularly reviewing and adjusting your goals as needed.

Let these goals light your way, and may each step be taken with confidence and clarity.

Further picture in your mind's eye the life that awaits you once your financial goals are met. Can you feel the warmth of the sun as you stand on your new home's porch, the sense of accomplishment resonating in your chest? Visualization is a potent tool—a way to make your goals tangible even before they've been realized.

Let's consider the groundbreaking research by Dr. Gail Matthews, a psychology professor at the Dominican University of California. Her study on goal-setting strategies found that individuals who write down their goals, share them with a friend, and send weekly updates to that friend are on average 33% more successful in accomplishing their stated goals than those who merely formulate goals in their minds.

By vividly imagining your success, you fuel the fires of motivation. Create a vision board, if you can, a compilation of images that represent your goals. Place it where you'll see it daily as a constant reminder of the rewards that come from disciplined financial planning.

Guidelines to set your Professional Goals:

Professional goals are ones like becoming an engineer, a scientist, a singer, a musician, a doctor, an entrepreneur, a lawyer, a teacher, a nurse, a politician, etc. These goals will determine our financial earnings, our intellectual competency, and our role in our society, and the most important is that they will also determine the entire course of our lives. Hence, before we choose our goals, it is imperative that we analyse them carefully, as our professional goals will determine the direction, our growth, our stability, our rewards, and the entire future of our lives.

Please find below four different zones segregated according to four basic categories of professional work. The goal you chose will put you in one of these zones. These zones will give you a tentative idea of what kind of monetary achievements you will have and what the risks, rewards, competition, and overall stability of your life will be.

ZONE 4

Extraordinary people with Exceptional skills as Bill Gates, Warren Buffet, Steve Jobs.

Stability

Rewards

Growth

Recognition

Financial freedom

Skill development

Status

Extraordinary

ZONE 3

From General Manager to Directors, Presidents, highly educated and experienced people.

Stability

Rewards

Growth

Recognition

Financial freedom

Skill development

Status

Good

ZONE 2	
From a Sales person to Manager, generally educated and middle class including skilled workers.	
Stability	
Rewards	
Growth	
Recognition	Average
Financial freedom	
Skill development	
Status	

ZONE 1	
Labourers, People involved into physical labour with no special skills.	
Stability	
Rewards	
Growth	
Recognition	Poor
Financial freedom	
Skill development	
Status	

The above table outlines the basic factors associated with your professional and financial standing.

Zone 1: This zone is primarily for people who do physical work without any special skills. This zone does not require any special education or skills, and therefore most of the people who are not educated or skilled fall into this zone.

Let's examine some of the variables in this area.

- **Competition**: Severe, as anyone can enter this zone. No special qualification is required, making it easy to enter.

- **Stability**: Since anyone can enter anytime, there is no stability in this zone.

- **Rewards**: Since no special skills are required, returns are below average. Hence, a person in this zone will be poor and will struggle throughout his life. A lot of people in this zone are below the poverty line in most countries.

Similarly, other elements like growth, recognition, skill development, and status will be very low. There is no financial freedom in this zone.

Zone 2. This zone is basically for people with average skills, like having a degree in a bachelor of commerce, arts, engineering, lawyer, etc. Generally, all graduate people fall into Zone 2. It takes years for them to gain experience and come into Zone 3. Till that time, they remain in zone 2, and after they have passed more than half of their professional life, they acquire the ability to come into zone 3.

Let's examine some of the variables in this area.

- **Competition**: Severe. The population of people in this zone is tremendous. The required qualification is not very hard to achieve; hence, anyone can enter this zone easily.

- **Stability**: Since it is not very hard to be part of this zone and most of the masses come into this zone, there is no stability.

- **Returns**: Returns are just average. A person in this zone will have a hand-to-mouth life. He has to struggle a lot to get to zone 3. He will just manage to make both ends meet.

Similarly, other elements like growth, recognition, skill development, and status will be at an average level. There is no financial freedom in life.

Zone 3. This zone is basically for people with significant experience or expertise. People from zone 2 with a lot of experience and expertise may enter zone 3. This zone has people starting from General Managers to Presidents, CEOs, Entrepreneurs, etc. These people fall into a specialized category. They are people who hold a high level of importance in their fields and are highly competent. It is not easy to enter this zone. These are the class people of society and are in great demand. They are basically the experts and leaders in their field.

Let us analyse various factors in these zones.

- **Competition**: Lesser. The required skills are not very easy to achieve, making it difficult to enter this zone.

- **Stability**: Since a certain class becomes a part of this zone, stability is good.

- **Returns**: Returns are quite good. A person in this zone enjoys most of the good things of this world, like a good car, house, world tours, a high level of respect, etc. He is above the average person.

Similarly, other elements like growth, recognition, skill development, and status will be good. They can plan their financial freedom in life, and they have high chances of entering Zone 4.

Zone 4. This zone is primarily for highly extraordinary people or people with exceptional qualities. All the billionaires of the world fall into this category.

Let us analyse various factors in these zones.

- **Competition**: Very little. The required skills are not very easy to achieve, making it difficult to enter this zone.

- **Stability**: Since it is hard to be a part of this zone, only a limited class becomes a part of it; hence, stability is much better.

- **Returns**: Returns are extraordinary beyond imagination. A person in this zone enjoys most of the luxurious things in the world, like the most expensive cars, a mansion, private planes, luxury yachts etc. Persons in this zone are financially free. It requires a lot of hard work, focus, knowledge, and, most importantly, expertise in this zone. This zone is very sensitive and very demanding. This zone only respects merits and values.

Similarly, other elements like growth, recognition, skill development, and status will be excellent. These people are financially free. These people are beyond the caprices of luck. Associating with such people will be considered fortunate for others.

	Zone 1	Zone 2	Zone 3	Zone 4
Stability	Most Unstable	Unstable	Stable/ Unstable	Quite Stable
Competition	Most severe	Severe	Less Severe	Less
Rewards	Poor	Average	Good	Extraordinary
Growth	Poor	Average	Good	Extraordinary
Recognition	Poor	Average	Good	Extraordinary
Financial freedom	Not Possible	Difficult	Achievable	Easily achievable.
Skills	Poor	Average	Good	Exceptional
Status	Poverty Class	Middle Class	Rich Class	Extraordinarily Rich

Put your goals into the above zones and analyze whether the results meet your expectations. If they do not re-plan your goals.

Now let me come to the most important point of this Chapter.

"What is your Master piece Goal?"

Whenever I ask this question to people, they ask me what do I mean by a Master piece goal. I reply as follows.

A Master piece goal is a goal that serves as the blueprint of your life, represents your identity, empowers you, and makes your life meaningful by all means. A master piece goal is the one that makes you financially stable and strong, not someone else. A master piece goal is the one that fulfils your dreams and not someone else's. A master piece goal is a clear goal that works with your passion and strategy and turns into a legacy lasting for generations.

A master piece goal is the one that gives meaning to your life and is solely attributed to your hard work and skills; it is the one that rewards you adequately and aligns your personal aspirations and values with your professional accomplishments. It brings balance and harmony within all the different aspects of life, like family, business, health, wealth, spirituality, and other essential objectives for your overall well-being.

List out your dreams and check if you have any Master piece goal or if you are only engaging in trivial pursuits.

Without a Master piece goal, our life would be meaningless, our efforts will go in vain and all our achievements will be worthless. Before we move on to the next subject, kindly ask this important question to yourself.

"What is your Master piece goal?"

If you don't have, then determine your master piece goal, right now.

In Conclusion

Dear reader, setting and achieving financial goals is not merely a matter of numbers or statistics. It is a significant and life-affirming action that resonates with the deepest wishes of your heart. It's a commitment to live cautiously to shape a future of wealth and peace.

As we conclude this chapter, take a moment to contemplate the goals that will shape your financial roadmap. Embrace the journey with awareness, for each step you take is a step closer to the life you aspire to lead. Your goals are not just aspirations; they are the very architecture of success.

MOTIVATION

Motivation is the most important factor in pushing our vehicle to success. If there is no motivation, it will be difficult to reach our goals. Without motivation, we become dull and inactive. Basically, we are devoid of enthusiasm, which means mentally, we are incapacitated. Physically, we are healthy, but mentally, we are sick. The mind does not function to its fullest. It not only impacts our work but also creates a multitude of problems, such as reducing productivity and efficiency, amplifying procrastination, creating depression and a pessimistic outlook, and ultimately halting our progress entirely.

We often become lazy, and such laziness may easily sabotage our achievements.

Hence, as we decide our financial goals, we also need to motivate ourselves. Motivation will fill you with all the enthusiasm, courage, and strength required to cover the journey of success. However, to clarify this, I would like to first start with the basics.

Whatever work we do in our lives can be categorized into two segments.

1. Labour.
2. Devotion.

What is labour? Whatever work we do without enthusiasm in life is just labour.

What is devotion? All work done with enthusiasm and passion is devotion.

If a teacher in his class performs his duties without enthusiasm, his teaching will be all labour. However, for a worker who is passionate about placing bricks in the right order, as if he is constructing a Taj Mahal, his work is no less than devotion to God.

One day, a pious man was praying to God, "How shall I meditate upon you so that you can grace me with all your blessings?"

God said, "Go outside the church and see how the sweeper sweeps the road. When he sweeps, all the Gods and deities descend from the heavens in order to draw inspiration from his sweeping. If you have this kind of enthusiasm, nothing can stop me from bestowing my blessings upon you."

Most of the people in this world work without enthusiasm. They work only to the extent that they can survive in their jobs. The most serious problem in this world is not unemployment; it is the people who are employed but disengaged from their duties and responsibilities because they do not have the enthusiasm and passion to work. There is no fragrance of zeal in their work. Such type of work is called "labour." In this world, we have plenty of such labourers at various levels, e.g., CEOs of companies, managers, senators, presidents, salesmen, doctors, lawyers, employees, employers, etc.

I have seen people coming to the office in the morning, but there is no zeal within them. When you ask them to work, they feel burdened. They get irritated. There is no sense of responsibility within them. They make excuses, and they suck up your time and energy, and finally, they become a liability. Their life is a never-ending struggle.

Hence, enthusiasm is the fundamental quality that leads to increased productivity, positivity, and overall well-being.

As I say in my Quotes:

"To get up early in the morning is not enough,

To get up with enthusiasm is more important."

Enthusiasm multiplies when we feel motivated in our lives. For example, a very typical example is how people feel in their office on Monday and how they feel on Friday. All over the world, people feel dull on Mondays, and they are much more excited on Fridays. Their excitement on Friday is clearly attributed to their motivation stemming from the upcoming weekend.

So, one of the main reasons we do not feel enthusiastic is a lack of motivation. We all need motivation. No matter how knowledgeable a person may be, if he does not feel motivated, all his knowledge will be of no use in his life. Hence, motivation becomes an important factor. Motivation will decide how fast we will reach our goals.

Therefore, let us go on this expedition of motivation.

Generally, Motivation is classified into two categories:

1. Internal Motivation

2. External Motivation

Most people say that motivation should be internal and not external. In fact, motivation comes only from within ourselves.

"Motivation is igniting your spirit that comes from the core of your heart, producing a wave with all the enthusiasm, which is impossible to be resisted by any external force, and keeping you working consistently, till the time your goals are achieved."

How to ignite your motivation: To ignite motivation, we need a source. This source is called as the X-factor. This source can be internal or external.

For example, to someone, money can be motivating, but to someone, recognition may be motivating; to someone, his poverty may be motivating, but to someone, higher goals may be motivating; sometimes a good experience can be motivating, but sometimes a bad experience can be motivating; sometimes love can be motivating, but sometimes pain can be motivating. For every individual, this motivation factor is different, and until we do not touch this X-factor, it is difficult to motivate him. Hence, most of the time, people fail to motivate people because they use the same X-factor for everyone. Unless we touch this X factor specifically for a specific individual, we will be unable to motivate him effectively.

Unfortunately, most people hardly know their X factor. This X-factor can be anything. Go deep within yourself and locate your X-factor. List all those things that you think trigger your mind and motivate you. I am highlighting some of the X-factors in case they can help motivate you:

1. A nice house, a luxurious car, and exotic world tours.

2. Financial freedom in life.

3. Retirement at the age of 50, not 60.

4. Live your life for yourself and not for someone else's dreams.

5. No more alarm clocks to wake up in the morning.

6. Recognition in society.

7. Set your life as an example for others.

8. Your friend's statement that you are good for nothing - prove it wrong.

9. Be your own boss and not a slave to others.

10. Complete freedom in life.

What do you cherish? What ignites your spirit? Give a deep thought and find it now.

Once you find your X-factor, harness the power of visualization. Imagine yourself standing at the pinnacle of your financial dreams, with a panoramic view of your accomplishments unfolding before you. Now just check how do you feel. Do you feel excited. Do you feel motivated. If yes then surround yourself with your X-factor.

Multiple research and stories have demonstrated how this practice of visualization has empowered ordinary people to become extraordinary.

Furthermore, the process of visualization, which involves picturing oneself along with his financial dreams, activates the brain areas linked to decision-making and cognitive functioning. This mental simulation prepares the mind to identify and take advantage of opportunities essential for realizing one's financial goals. As a result, we have a better probability of succeeding when opportunities arise.

Further visualization fuels motivation and clarity, while goal-setting acts as a roadmap for action. Together, they create a synergy that propels individuals towards their financial objectives, not through wishful thinking but through inspired action.

In conclusion, the journey towards financial prosperity is not a path walked in the dark. Visualization lights the way, while goal-setting lays down the stones upon which we tread. This powerful combination is a proven method for achieving financial goals. Hence, use the power of visualization, and you will experience a tremendous surge of inspiration resulting from this phenomenon.

During my discussion with my father about motivation he said, "Sometimes a negative connotation is more effective in life than a positive inspiration."

He gave some examples, and this is quite true. I would like to share one example with you.

In May 1893, while Mahatma Gandhi was on his way to Pretoria, a white man objected to Gandhi's presence in a first-class carriage, and he was ordered to move at the end of the train in a third-class compartment. Gandhi, who had a first-class ticket, refused, but was thrown off the train at Pietermaritzburg. It was a bitterly cold night as he moved into the dark waiting room of Maritzburg station, shivering through the night. But something happened to him in the waiting room of Maritzburg railway station under the insult inflicted on him. He considered this encounter to be one of the most creative experiences of his life. From that hour, he refused to accept injustice in South Africa.

Later on, the NEWS came as under:

"Mahatma Gandhi is ejected from a South African train, motivating him to fight for Indian rights in the British colony."

Gandhi made the momentous decision to stay in South Africa and fight the racial discrimination against Indians there. Out of that struggle emerged his unique version of Nonviolent Resistance and Satyagraha. He fought with determination against the British and succeeded.

Today, a bronze statue of Gandhi stands on Church Street in the city centre in Pietermaritzburg.

Sometimes, when positive emotions or rewards fail, the negative experiences prove to be stronger. In case of God, this is very true. People remember God only when they are in pain or when they need something. When they are confronted with challenges and failures, or when they are unable to accomplish something, they pray to God.

Hence, if you are unable to find your X-factor from positive rewards, try to find it from negative connotations in a positive way.

Further, I would like to highlight one more important thing. As you try to find positive motivation in this world, you will find people, events, or circumstances demotivating you. Most of the time, you will find more demotivating factors than motivating factors in your life. Unfortunately, the most tragic thing is that we take the demotivating factors more seriously than the motivating factors in our lives. We are more influenced by negativity than positivity. One negative statement will keep echoing in our ears and will have a tremendous cascading effect on our mindset. This will then require enormous positive conditioning to help us recover. Hence, before we motivate ourselves, we should keep ourselves away from demotivating factors.

Further, I would like to share a recent conversation I had with my friend. He was complaining to me, "In our company, there is no motivation, no appreciation. The management does not care how hard we work. How do you expect me to perform in such an environment?"

My reply was very simple. I said, "You can still deliver results the way an Indian cricket team, while playing in Pakistan, still wins the match despite having no motivation in the stadium."

Just imagine when an Indian cricket team plays in Pakistan. The moment they hit a six, there is no clapping. On the contrary, there is absolute silence. Despite all the motivational factors being absent in the stadium, they still play with a spirit to win the match because their motivation is not external; it is internal. They know they are playing for their country, and this internal motivation inspires them to win the match. They do not care if anyone claps for them or not, but they still perform because their internal motivation is quite strong. Hence, when your external circumstances are not supportive, make yourself internally strong and motivate yourself internally.

Hence, no matter whether we receive or do not receive any appreciation in our company or in this world from our friends or relatives, we have to perform and we have to win. This is how we become self-motivated. A successful person is self-motivated. We have to find our X-factor, and no matter what circumstances we face, we shall not give up until we achieve our goals.

Remember, the future belongs to those who believe in the beauty of their dreams and set forth with determination and clarity towards making them a reality. Faith and motivation are your allies on this journey, equipping you with the vision to see the goals and the resolve to achieve it.

Motivation is the driving force that enables you to continually exert effort, work passionately, and keep you going strong and stable while facing your challenges. Hence find your X-factor, fuel yourself and keep moving till the time you don't achieve your financial goals.

THE FUNDAMENTAL PRINCIPLES OF BUSINESS

Once, I was sitting with one of my friends, named Dheeraj. We used to meet occasionally. He belonged to Marwari community. Marwari Community is a community from the state known as Rajasthan in India. They are an enterprising community having a deep understanding about finance and Investments. As entrepreneurs, and business leaders, the community has a great contribution to the economy of the nation. We Indians are proud to have such enterprising people, from whom there is a lot to learn about business and money matters.

Dheeraj was an entrepreneur. He always admired my communication abilities, technical expertise, and my ability to analyse concepts and philosophies related to life, wealth, and other subjects.

One day he told me, "Sukhvinder, though you are working just as a manager right now, but the kind of skills you have, believe me, you can easily get a job of General Manager or Vice President in any multinational organisation."

I replied to him and said, "Dheeraj, with the kind of calibre you have, you can earn all the wealth within one month, which I shall earn in a year after becoming a General manager or a Vice President of a multinational organisation."

He regarded my remark with a grin, taking it as a joke.

After a few years, I was promoted to the position of General Manager at the firm where I was employed. When I met him at that point of time, he had just bought a new brand car in cash without any loan, the cost of which was equivalent to my one-year salary as a General manager.

At that time, I told him, "Dheeraj, the basic difference between you and me is "**I know how to work well, whereas you know how to earn well.**"

Out of curiosity, I asked him about business, and he shared the ten principles of business, which are quite interesting.

1. Focus on turnover, reduce your profit margins, and reduce overhead costs.

2. Spend less and invest more.

3. Deal in cash (Immediate payment) rather than credits if you want to earn money fast.

4. Financial security is more important than profitability.

5. Appoint honest and competent people in your business, retain them, and reward them properly.

6. Work with a vision of the future; don't work blindly.

7. Do not compromise business time with your personal priorities.

8. Keep upgrading and diversifying your business.

9. People are the assets, not machines; experienced people are greater assets.

10. Maintain a low profile in life. Don't show off. Keep your personal expenses as low as possible.

Finally, after an extensive conversation with Dheeraj, I learned a very important aspect about money. We were talking about jobs and businesses. In conclusion, I learned from my discussion with Dheeraj, that jobs generally provide you with money just for your survival, but to become rich, you need to have your own business. A job will always tend to make you work well, whereas business will always compel you to earn well. Hence, if you want to become a multi-millionaire, plan for your own business.

I would like to share an important quote with regard to my discussions with Dheeraj.

What is the basic difference between an Employee and an Employer?

A good Employee knows how to **"Work well."**

Whereas a good Employer knows how to **"Earn well."**

The above answer is simple, and the below fact is also simple.

Education teaches us to **"Work well,"** but

Life compels us to **"Earn well."**

VALUES

This book is more than just a collection of concepts; it is a guide designed to lead you towards a more fulfilling engagement with wealth. It is a meticulously crafted manual intended to redefine success and shift the focus from mere acquisition to purposeful achievement. Here, we explore not only how to make more money but also how to make money more meaningful.

In a world where success is often measured by the size of one's wallet, we risk losing sight of the values that make life truly worth living. The pursuit of wealth, devoid of purpose, is a voyage to nowhere. It leaves us stranded in the shallow waters of materialism, far from the depths of fulfilment.

In this context I recall a story of a person who was poor and uneducated and still managed to become a multimillionaire.

This is another intriguing story about an individual named Ravi, who worked as an assistant to an electrician. For a few years, he has been working in our area, and I used to see him often on a bicycle, toiling day and night like a worker. However, after fifteen years, when I met him, I was extremely astounded to know about his achievements. He had become a multimillionaire.

It was a marriage ceremony where he had come, and he recognised me right away. He called me by my nickname, as he knew me when I was quite young, in my adolescence. Since his entire personality was changed, I could barely recognise him. Basically, he was a person with no education; he worked as a helper to an electrician; and he had a poor family background. But looking at his outfit and the confidence in his tone, I could figure out that he was no longer that poor Ravi. During our conversation, I came to know that he is the owner of a few factories. While leaving the parking area, I was surprised to see his Audi S4. I was once again curious to know about his successful journey.

Hence, I asked him, "Ravi, how did you accomplish all of this?"

He smiled and said, "It's all the grace of God."

I said, "I appreciate your humility Ravi, but I am keen to know about your journey of such significant accomplishments."

I insisted and finally, I invited him for dinner, and he agreed. On my insistence, he also agreed to share his journey of success.

As agreed, we met in a quaint restaurant nestled on the outskirts of the city. It was during the weekday; hence, there was no rush. It was a perfect place to sit and listen. Ravi started with his story. As I listened intently, my mind was ablaze with insights. His journey was not a linear path but an interesting endeavour of involvement, excellence, and commitment to values. I will share his story in his own words.

He said, "Sukhvinder, you know I was a helper to Mr. Manish, who I would say was a skilled electrician. I worked with several skilled people, and I observed that the majority of them lacked the following:

1. **Lack of commitment**: The first thing these people lack is "Commitment." For example, they will promise to come at 9:00 a.m. to do the job, but they will never come on time. Then you phone them, and either they will not come, giving some lame excuse, or they will come very late.

2. **Lack of tools and equipment**: Most of the skilled people lack proper tools and equipment. For example, most electricians don't have clamp meters. This meter accurately displays the current value, voltage value, resistance value, and continuity, making it a crucial tool for any electrician. However, the

majority do not possess this. Similarly, trained professionals such as carpenters, air conditioning repairers, and plumbers they will never have the necessary equipment to carry out a quality job. Without proper equipment, people are bound to compromise on the quality of work.

3. **Lack of precision**: They do not have the ability to do the job with precision and accuracy. They do not work on the details. They just want to finish the work somehow. For e.g., if you ask any electrician to install a concealed box, he will not have a level gauge and when you try to fix the main plate, you need different sizes of screws, because the box is misaligned from all four sides. Again, this happens with all the skilled workers. They lack precision in their work. This results in a substandard job.

4. **Careless approach**: The majority of skilled workers don't give a damn about their surroundings, while doing their job. They leave their workspace messy after finishing their work. They do not care about what they have done around them as long as they have been successful in completing their work. Therefore, it's similar to finishing a task and then giving the owner a new one. As a result, the owner has to start cleaning and fixing the mess they made in their immediate area as soon as they depart.

5. **People don't update their skills**: The way technology is changing; skilled workers do not update themselves. They do not update their knowledge, and they become obsolete. Most people think they know everything, but their knowledge is outdated within a few years. They pretend to know everything, and this attitude makes them professionally unfit, and they keep struggling to work proficiently in their entire lives.

With the above five weaknesses, the quality of job gets compromised, and the job done is substandard. Clients will never be satisfied. Consequently, they fail to earn goodwill in their profession, which is crucial for growth in business.

Hence these individuals don't advance too far in their profession. I feel sorry to say that they keep struggling throughout their lives and are unable to achieve success beyond a certain threshold.

These are the five fundamental deficiencies that I identified in many skilled workers. Furthermore, these individuals do not acknowledge their shortcomings. As a result, they fail to learn and improve. But I learned and made the following improvements:

1. Have commitment in life.

2. Have all the required tools and equipment to carry out a high-quality job.

3. Work with precision.

4. Ensure your job does not spoil someone else's.

5. Update your knowledge and skills consistently.

The most important thing was customer satisfaction. Good relationships can transform a one-time buyer into a lifelong patron. Hence it is important that we handle clients with empathy and efficiency. Business is not just about selling products; it's about building relationships, about creating a community of customers who return not merely for what you sell, but for how you sell.

Due to the above improvements and the values which I believed; my work became outstanding. I don't boast, but there was no one who could carry out the job as per my standards. My business started growing simply with references. I was never short of work.

Apart from the above, I constantly updated my knowledge. To put it simply, if you want to really learn, you learn either from your experience or from experts. Experience is a good teacher, but it is a slow teacher. If you rely on your experience, then your success will be inordinately delayed. As a result, I learned from the experts and read all the books recommended by them. I attended paid courses where experts came and taught. Eventually, the horizon and potential of my business expanded, and very soon my business started growing.

Within 3 years, my business was out of my reach. Now there was a need for a drastic change, and I realised that if I keep doing things on my own, I won't be able to grow. So, there was a need to scale my business and build up a good team. It was clear that I needed to recruit new people. Recruiting new people was not a problem, but making them work as per my standards was a challenge. My goal was to expand my business without compromising the quality or values that have brought this venture to its current standing. Business expansion is not merely about increasing sales; it's about enhancing your capacity to handle an expanding workload without compromising quality or customer satisfaction. It is a delicate balancing act that requires foresight and strategic planning.

Hence, I recruited new people, and I gave them all the tools and equipment. I provided them with all the guidelines and protocols. Despite all my efforts, they did not work as per my standards. My work was getting compromised. Despite all my attempts, these people never obeyed me. They never went on time. I kept chasing them on behalf of my customers, but they did the same thing—what they have been doing their entire lives. Hence, getting work done by these people as per my expectations was a big challenge. If you become harsh, they will leave you immediately. You can't do anything against them. I became helpless.

I was stuck. There was no way I could expand my business. There was no way I could change these people's attitude.

If I had to maintain the quality of my work, I would have to work myself. So, there was no way I could move ahead.

My journey was fraught with challenges and it required more than just hard work; it required an effective strategy for advancement.

However, I didn't give up. One Sunday morning, I went to the office and did some statistics.

I listed the names of all those people who had worked for me in the last one year. I assessed everyone's work and gave them markings pertaining to their job quality, commitment, skills, attitude, and willingness to learn and improve. I gave them ratings for each specific activity and prepared a comprehensive report. After doing the analysis, I found that most of the young people, though they were less experienced and knowledgeable, were more obedient and easier to mold. They had a learning attitude. They were ready to change and improve. People who were old and experienced had become adamant, and it was difficult to change them. Hence, I filtered the list of people who were working with me. I let go of those people who were difficult to change, and I continued with the ones who were willing to adapt and improve. Similarly, I started recruiting new people in my firm, and I gave priority to attitude rather than experience and knowledge. I established a recruitment process that attracted talent aligned with our vision and values.

In order to groom new people, I made formal procedures for most of the jobs so that the job quality does not get compromised. These procedures dictated how a particular task or process should be carried out in a systematic and organized manner to ensure consistency, efficiency, and compliance with the required standards. I trained my staff to the best of my ability.

Basically, I ensured that my team is equipped, both in skills and mindset. Investing in training and development is not a luxury; it's a necessity.

After training we continuously monitored their work with respect to their commitments, job quality, compliance with our procedures and standards.

It was always our goal to maintain the quality of our work and deliver more than the customer's expectations.

As we maintained our quality, we were never short of work. Initially, we were doing work only for residential projects, but gradually we started working for industries, for powerhouses, for telecommunications, etc. We do everything now. Maintaining the core values on which my company was built, my business was growing abundantly. In a short span of time, I achieved significant progress.

Gradually as my knowledge widened, I diversified my business and came into manufacturing sector from service segment. I started manufacturing control panels initially and then electrical wires. Later on, we started exporting, and now we are also importing a lot of engineering equipment and selling in the domestic market. My business has now grown to millions.

Sukhvinder, I have shared with you my story in a brief and simple manner, but this journey was not that easy. This journey was fraught with challenges, and at every step, I had to fight without letting myself get discouraged. I never gave up, remained steadfast in the values I believed in, and kept pursuing until I achieved my goals. I always had the passion to deliver nothing less than "**Excellence**."

I asked him, "Ravi, what do you think is the most important factor that contributes to your success?"

He said, "**First** are values. Don't compromise on values. **Second**, always strive for excellence—nothing less than that. **Third**, in order to achieve excellence, keep learning; learning is a continuous process, not just a one-time task. **Fourth**, improvement and upgrading yourself. **Fifth**, focus on the growth of your organization. However, without the growth of the employees, an organization will never grow. Hence, empower your employees with knowledge, skills, and rewards."

These five things have been the cornerstone of my success story. I call them my "Value Management System."

It was again a very enlightening experience with Ravi. Reflecting on Ravi's journey, we glean valuable insights. His success was underpinned by a willingness to grow and a relentless focus on values.

It is a narrative that intertwines values, vision and commitment. It's a journey of constant learning, knowing your customer, and delivering to the best of your abilities. Ravi's success was not a product of mere hardwork but of strategic, genuine engagement. The pursuit of money, when anchored in purpose and passion, can be an endeavour, a means to make a significant difference in the world. It's a path that requires commitment, involvement, and a willingness to challenge conventional way of doing business to an entirely new level where the job quality is not guaranteed upto 99.99% but 100%.

In conclusion, I learned that the foundation of all success stories is laid on great values. When you cultivate values, you are bound to be successful and your success will be long lasting.

In this financial world, the good news is that there is tremendous scope for earning money. The only thing we need is a strong will and commitment.

I remember my experience with a plumber who was doing some repairs at my neighbour's house. Coincidentally, I met him when he was finishing his job and about to leave. I assigned him the task of replacing one of my taps in my garden. He did the job. It was the month of October, when the Diwali festival was approaching. Diwali is a festival in India, like Christmas in the West, celebrated with a lot of vibrance and vigor. While the plumber was finishing his job, I was telling my son that there were three pending jobs in our house that we needed to complete before Diwali. One was a small welding job; the other was some carpentry work; and the third was an electrical job.

While conversing with my son, the plumber overheard me, and within a trice he said, "Sir, I have a welder, I have an electrician, and

I have a carpenter also working with me. I can get all three jobs done for you."

I showed him all the jobs and asked, "When can you bring those people?"

He said, "I will bring them tomorrow, and since it's a small job, we shall finish by tomorrow."

I said, "Fine."

We exchanged our phone numbers, and I also agreed on a price for all three jobs that he offered without any negotiation.

The next day, I was waiting for him, but he didn't show up.

I tried to call him, but there was no response. Finally, I got the job done by someone else.

Later, after a month, I met him and asked why he did not show up as promised, and he gave me all kinds of lame excuses.

Well, this experience was not something new. It happens a lot of the time.

The moral of the story is that this person had all the resources at his disposal; he knew a good carpenter, an electrician, and a welder and had a good opportunity to earn, but still he failed. The question is why did he fail? What did he lack?

The answer is simple. He lacked commitment in life. He did not fulfil his promise. I have observed individuals who exhibit great enthusiasm while talking, but while coming into action, they become totally dull. This is what happens in everyone's life. We all lack the basic quality, i.e., "Commitment."

This world is full of resources and opportunities; what we need is commitment to act and execute. They way we dream or talk, we need to have the same enthusiasm while we work. Action is the key to progress, and commitment is the key to making ourselves act.

Money is not hard to earn; it is hard only to begin and then remain persistent and consistent. The one who determines and remains steady will achieve. Moreover, as per my experience, I can affirm that when you aim at millions, you will always receive much beyond that. Hence, think big and act fast.

AGE IS NO BARRIER

In the journey of human life, age often serves as a measure of the physical energy depleting with time. Apparently, our mental capabilities are often analysed with our physical strength. But actually, when it comes to financial success, age is merely a number, not a barrier. The journey to wealth and fulfilment knows no age limit.

It is obvious that age brings a wealth of experience, not limitations. Every year provides us with a deeper understanding of the world and ourselves. With time, our knowledge is empowered by our experience. Our experiences, which are marked by failures, relentless pursuit, and eventual triumphs, have shaped the experts within us. Such expertise did not come from textbooks or classrooms but from the gritty, hands-on challenges of the real world. Eventually, with age, we become not the ordinary but the extraordinary human beings.

Hence, as far as financial achievements are concerned, there is no age restrictions. Consider the stories of those who defied the age norm. Colonel Sanders founded Kentucky Fried Chicken in his sixties. Grandma Moses, who began her painting career in her late seventies. Their successes were not mere accidents but the results of passion, resilience, and the refusal to let age define their capabilities.

I would like to narrate the story of KFC in brief as follows:

1. The founder of KFC was Colonel Harland Sanders.

2. Colonel Harland was born in 1890 in Henryville.

3. His father passed away when he was six years old. Sanders had to cook and take care of his two younger siblings.

4. In seventh grade, at the age of 13, he dropped out of school and left home to go work as a farmhand.

5. At 16, he faked his age to enlist in the United States Army. After being honourably discharged a year later, he got hired by the Railways as a labourer. However, he got fired for fighting with a coworker.

6. While he worked for the Railways, stoking the fire and managing the steam, he studied law—until he ruined his legal career by getting into another fight.

7. Eventually, Sanders was forced to move back with his mom and get a job selling life insurance. He again got fired for insubordination.

8. His 20s and 30s were a series of failed jobs and unsuccessful ventures.

9. He launched his first startup at the age of 30—a ferry boat service over the Ohio River. Unfortunately, a bridge built nearby rendered his services redundant.

10. His next venture was an oil lamp business, which also failed due to competition and other external factors.

11. At the age of 37, Sanders took charge of a Standard Oil gas station in Nicholasville, Kentucky, but with the slump of the Great Depression, he was forced to close within 3 years.

12. At age 40, he opened his second service station that same year, in Corbin, Kentucky, where he started selling his homemade chicken to truck drivers for a bit of extra cash, but eventually got closed down due to an argument with a local competitor, which resulted in a deadly shootout.

13. After four years, Sanders purchased another filling station on the other side of the road. By 1936, this had proven successful enough for Sanders to be given the honorary title of Kentucky

Colonel by Governor Ruby Laffoon. In 1937, he expanded his restaurant to 142 seats, naming it Sanders's Café. Two years later, the restaurant was destroyed by fire.

14. Shortly after the fire, at the age of 49, construction began on the present Sanders Café, along with the addition of a motel. At this time, Sanders was almost fifty years of age. Business continued to boom as it was located along the main highway. However, due to a split in the highway route, resulting in the bypassing of the motel, business fell down, and eventually Sanders sold the café in 1956. He was just left with a $105 social security check to his name at the age of 65.

15. However, during the setbacks, Sanders kept improving his chicken recipe, finally creating what came to be known as his "Original Recipe" of 11 herbs and spices.

16. At the age of 65, he set out to sell his franchised chicken model to restaurants across the country. He travelled town to town, door to door, all across the country, in his old car, pitching his recipe. At times, he was so broke that he actually lived in his old car. He did this for two years, and he still had no takers. He was rejected by 1,009 people before one agreed to his idea, and then everyone knows the story.

In 1964, he had more than 600 franchises, including overseas franchises in Canada, the UK, Mexico, and Jamaica. Finally, he sold the Kentucky Fried Chicken Corporation for $2 million, along with some other benefits, as a salaried brand ambassador.

At age 90, Sanders passed away. At that time, there were around 6,000 KFC locations in 48 countries. In 2023, they had 26,000 restaurants in 150 countries.

When most people think of retiring, this man sets out with the new goal of establishing franchisees with his secret recipe for fried chicken. Despite facing multiple rejections and disappointments, he was determined, persistent, and consistent, and finally he succeeded.

If you're overwhelmed by rejection or disheartened by setbacks, remember the story of Colonel Harland Sanders. He was fired from multiple jobs, failed in his legal career, went down due to the Great Depression and World War II, but still created one of the largest fast-food chains in the world. It was the indomitable spirit of Colonel Harland Sanders that did not let him down, and he pursued his goals steadily and unremittingly.

He is a great inspiration to everyone. He has proved that age is no barrier, and one should never stop trying because of failure and rejection. It is never too late to build your valuable dreams.

CONCLUSION

The pursuit of wealth is a journey, not just of the wallet, but of the heart and mind. It's about taking control of one's financial destiny, about crafting a career that blends passion with profit, about the empowerment that comes from a positive mindset.

Through disciplined savings, prudent spending, and strategic investment, an individual can not only secure but also thrive in their financial standing.

Some people say this world is an illusion, some say it is full of distractions; some say it is full of opportunities. I agree with everyone.

For people who do not have the right knowledge, this world is an illusion.

For people who have a weak mindset, this world is full of distractions.

And for people who have valuable skills and expertise, this world is full of opportunities.

In closing, let me share the fact with you.

As per the Credit Suisse report, the wealth of this world is increasing day by day. The global household wealth totalled approximately USD 194.5 trillion in mid-2010, and it was approximately USD 463.6 trillion by the end of 2021. Increased by over two-fold in a mere 11 years. It doesn't matter what happens in this world—whether it is hit by pandemics, wars, recessions, political breakdowns, global warming, etc.— it remains indisputable that wealth is steadily growing and benefiting those who possess valuable skills.

An eminent advantage of the contemporary era is that even a poor person can become rich, and the speed with which he can become rich was never before.

According to the Credit Suisse Global Wealth Report 2022, the global population of millionaires is projected to increase by 40% over the next five years. By 2026, there will be more than 87.5 million people with at least $1 million in wealth, a significant increase from the 62.5 million recorded in 2021.

Hence, it is up to you whether you are prepared to take the advantage or not. As mentioned earlier the world is not waiting; it is hurtling forward, and to stand still is to fall behind. Hence it is time to act fast and thing big.

I trust that the profound revelations in this book have given you the clarity and wisdom you seek. As you embark on this journey, let the insights within these pages serve as a potential guide at every step. With each step forward, you are not only enhancing your financial well-being but also empowering financial freedom for yourself and building a legacy for your loved ones.

The journey isn't always smooth; there will be storms to weather and doldrums to endure. But the destination—a life of financial freedom—is worth every challenge. Embrace the journey, for each step brings you closer to the zenith of financial freedom.

So, I urge you, dear readers, to take these principles and mold them with the clay of your ambitions. Let them be the foundation upon which you build your empire of wealth.